Ukraine-Germany-Russia

The Weberian Alternative to Stefan Bollinger's 'The Russians are Coming!'

Publications

Leibniz contra Westphalia (2015)

G.W. Leibniz: Double Revolution and *Praefatio* (2015)

Immanuel Kant and the Mastication of Poland (2017)

Kant's Political Testament (2018)

Niklas Luhmann's Metatheoretical Systems Theory of Law (2018)

The Political Biography of the Young Leibniz in the Age of Secret Diplomacy, 2nd Ed. (2018)

Kant and Poland No. 3. Notes to the Dark Side of Kant's Cosmopolitanism (2019)

G.W. Leibniz: East-West Fusion and the End of Absolutist Sovereignty. Russophilia Continuity from Leibniz to Kant (2019)

Max Weber & The Slavs (2019)

German Philosophy Materials 2006-2014, Vols. I & II (2020)

Kant's Sovereignty Ruses (2022)

The Peace of Utrecht. Origins of Neo-Chinggisid International Relations Structures 1713-1998 (2022)

Ukraine-Germany-Russia

The Weberian Alternative to Stefan Bollinger's 'The Russians are Coming!'

William F. Drischler

Copyright © William F. Drischler, 2023

All rights reserved.

ISBN: 9798392828715

First published April 2023

Cover illustrations: Map of Ukraine, March 2023;
Max Weber, 1864-1920

BISAC: Philosophy/Political

For months the [Ukrainian] front has been frozen. It reminds us of the Western front in 1916.

Jürgen Habermas, "A Pleas for Negotiations," in the *Suddeutsche Zeitung*, Feb. 14, 2023

France feared Germany [prior to 1914] because its population and industry were growing faster, so it made an alliance with Russia, on the far side of Germany. Germany felt encircled and made an alliance with Austria-Hungary, which wanted German backing because it was competing with Russia for . . . territory in the Balkans. And Britain made an "entente" with France and Russia because it also felt threatened by the rise of Germany.

Gwynne Dyer,
The Shortest History of War,
2nd Printing 2022, p. 130

The Russian state's dependence on foreign finance capital . . . is a theme that weaves its way throughout .. . Weber's ... whole . . . 'Pseudo-Constitutionalism' essay [1906].

"Editors' Introduction" to Max Weber. The Russian Revolutions, Gordon C. Wells and Peter Baehr, Eds., 1997, p. 9

.

Weber's claim . . . is that Russia's mobilization in 1914, and with it the entire Tsarist system, bears the main responsibility for the outbreak of the Great War.

Karl Palonen, "The Supranational Dimension in Max Weber's Vision of Politics," in E. Hanke, et al, The Oxford Handbook of Max Weber, 2019, pp. 266-267

Sonya Zekri's harrowing report on the front (*Suddeutsche Zeitung*, Feb. 2, 2023) . . . is indeed reminiscent of depictions of the horror of the western front in 1916.

Habermas, "A Plea for Negotiations," etc.

SUMMARY
OF
CONTENTS

I. Stefan Bollinger's Model of Germany in the Era of the Great War, 1914-1919.

German imperialism, fueled by raw materials hunger, cultural militarism and broadly popular enthusiasm for annexations under the leadership of rapacious capitalist industrialists and bankers, attacks Russia – perpetual object of Teutonic aggression and expansion lust - and Eastern and Western Europe as well, but the Western 'democracies' led by Britain and France (and eventually joined by the U.S.) foil the Germans' well-laid plans.

II. Max Weber's Model of Germany in the Era of the Great War, 1914-1919

Russian "People's Imperialism" (*Volksimperialismus*), a 'nakedly expansionist' and 'absolutely undemocratic' tendency embodying the purest militarism on the planet while being fueled by 'culture deficit' derived Slavic peasant land hunger and egged on by the Czarist/Great Russian chauvinist Sino-Mongol (Chinggisid) bureaucracy; Orthodox State Church fanaticism; and Russia's teutophobic pseudo-intelligentsia – as well as a 'despotic' governing elite seeking to distract attention from domestic social problems through resort to war - launches an encirclement attack upon peace-loving Germany and Austria-Hungary, the 'constant Russian threat' manifesting itself via an 'iron' undemocratic regime bankrolled every step of the way by Anglo-Saxon capital forces actively overseeing their St. Petersburg 'debtor state' as undergirded by French *revanchiste* ('Russian vassal') elements. Such was the nature of the 'terrible threat' to Germany (and Western civilization) (and 'the culture of the whole world') Russian 'expansion drive' despotism and its patrons had by 1917 posed for 'decades;' namely: the prospect of 'installation of Russian conditions' throughout Central Europe, i.e.,'the absolute domination of St. Petersburg and Moscow' accomplished via deployment of secret government steered street gangs, following Weber.

III. The Russian Federation in Ukraine, 2014-2023

Aggressor? Or victim of Anglo-Saxon capital globalist encirclement à la Germany in WWI?

Illustrations

	Page No.
Europe in August, 1914	20
The Bucharest Nine Encirclement of the Russian Federation in 2023	29

CONTENTS

Summary of Contents

Illustrations

Preface

I. Stefan Bollinger's Model of Germany in the Era of the Great War, 1914-1919

    Introduction
    Section Abstract
    Preliminary Review of Bollinger and the Outbreak of the Great War

II. Max Weber's Model of Germany in the Era of the Great War, 1914-1919

    a. Russia-Prussia Analogies, following Weber
    b. Weber on the Historical Specificity of the Rise of Western Liberalism and its Inapplicability to 20th Century Russia
    c. Weber's Thesis of incomparable Imperialism and Aggressiveness of Russia as a determinative Factor in the Outbreak of WWI
    d. The Anglo-Saxon Capital World Hegemony Network – a Weberian Reconstruction
        i Hegemony
        ii Anglo-Saxon Capital
    Max Weber Section Summary

EXCURSUS. Weber's Thesis the February 1917 Revolution in Russia was simply 'the Elimination of an incapable Monarch' and no Revolution. Laying the groundwork for Lenin's Wall Street 'Re-Russification' (de-Occidentalization) plan for October 1917

III. The Russian Federation in Ukraine, 2022-2023
    a. Stefan Bollinger's Rapallo Treaty Analogy
    b. Is Anglo-Saxon Hegemony doomed?
        i Multi-Polarity Proliferation
        ii BRICS De-dollarization accelerates Anglo-Saxon Decline

FINAL REVIEW & CONCLUSIONS

Appendix. "Oriental Despotism and August 1914," from *The Appeal to Reason. A Social-Democratic Quarterly*, No. 25, Spring 1980 (Walnut Creek, California)

Works Cited

Afterword. Species Boost and Hegemony Loss Anxiety

PREFACE

The second year of the Russian Federation special military action in Ukraine begun in February of 2022, the roots of which go back to the U.S.-backed Maidan coup d'état (and Odessa massacre) of 2014 resulting in autonomy strivings in Donbass and other regions of Ukraine, events which in turn eventually led to separatist movements there, is now under way.

Of considerable use in coming to an understanding of the situation (including in ways not understood by its author) is the 2022 work of German political scientist Stefan Bollinger, The Russians are Coming! (*Die Russen kommen!*). Bollinger serves as a cultural officer of the Party of the Left currently represented in the German Bundestag. Although the Party of the Left fell below the 5% vote minimum usually required for party representation in the German federal legislative body in the 2022 election, it benefited from several direct mandates victories – above all in Berlin - which allowed it to remain a federally-certified party in Germany for the time being.

Bollinger's work is marked by a very suggestive general hypothesis (that the state of affairs in Germany in the era of World War I can serve as a basis for understanding Russian actions in Ukraine today); a blatant political contradiction (Germany's allegedly inexcusable misconduct in starting and conducting World War I is similar to that of Russia in Ukraine today, but today's Russia should be forgiven anyway); and a thoroughly implausible series of contentions that warmongering Germany attacked its peace-loving neighbors on all sides in 1914 in order to steal raw minerals, attain state-egoistic glory and reach for world domination utilizing terrorist methods. Bollinger's general hypothesis was in any case confirmed in February 2023 by Jürgen Habermas.

In fact the respective situations of Germany in 1914 and Russia in 2023 are extraordinarily analogous, even if the analogy is fully comprehended by neither Bollinger nor Habermas. Both the respective countries were subjected to encirclement (*Einkreisung*) and attack by Anglo-Saxon globalist capital and its allies and minions, this owing to the accurate perception of the attackers in both cases that the social, economic and cultural accomplishments of their intended victims represented a threat to their global hegemony.

In the discussion to follow, Bollinger's contention that the analogy between the German situation in 1914 and the Russian situation today is an especially fruitful one for political analysis will be over-confirmed by showing his perspective on Germany in 1914 at times appears to be little more than an episode of Entente-Allied Teutophobic brainwashing.

Fortunately spade work for criticizing the Berlin political scientist's perspective on World War I era Germany is extensive and ready to hand. Social science legend Max Weber (1864-1920) was a participant observer in World War I and brought to bear unmatched comparative historical knowledge joined to thoroughgoing independence from Entente-Allied propaganda and myths about Germans and Germany. Weber's proofs Germany had been encircled and besieged by Anglo-Saxon capital and its Czarist Russian attack dog in 1914 provide a clear model for comprehending the encirclement and attack upon the Russian Federation conducted by Anglo-Saxon capital and its NATO attack dog today as embodied in the Bucharest Nine anti-Russian alignment, and as repeatedly described by current Russian Federation President Vladimir Putin.

In the following Bollinger's interpretation of Germany in the period of the First World War will be reconstructed, followed by a review of Weber's approach, especially the latter's distinctive interpretation of the February 1917 Russian Revolution and its consequences. The contradiction between Bollinger's assertion that alleged German aggression in 1914 was unforgivable but allegedly similar Russian aggression in Ukraine in Ukraine in 2022 should be forgiven, cannot be overlooked; this above and beyond the question of empirical validity of aggression characterizations in both scenarios. But however contradictory the internal structure of the argumentation in The Russians are Coming! may seem at times, two of its author's key methodological axioms – that the World War I situation is very promising for seeking analogies to the current situation in Eastern Europe, and that serious political discourse is always conducted in terms of historical analogies – are quite valid.

I. Stefan Bollinger's Model of Germany in the Era of the Great War, 1914-1919

INTRODUCTION. The discussion of Germany in the WWI era in Stefan Bollinger's *The Russians are Coming! How should we engage with the Ukraine War? On German Hysteria and its Causes* (2022)[1] departs as mentioned from the promising suggestion that current relations between Ukraine, Germany and Russia would be well understood by historically contextualizing them with reference to the German situation circa 1914. A closely related contention – that in order to properly understand the current Ukraine crisis, the reader should discard any notion that the current conflict in Eastern Europe is unprecedented or even highly unusual - is (as well be seen) also quite promising. Finally, Bollinger's judgment that making sense of a major conflict requires resort to historical analogies – even if any analogy has limitations – must be seconded.

Unfortunately, lurking between potentially fruitful method and solid results there lies a no man's land (to use a WWI expression) known as execution. In popular terms, the devil is in the details, and on a bewildering number of issues Bollinger's analysis is wrongheaded and/or implausible. Fortunately, his errors are closely knit together with clear steering misconceptions, allowing the reader to separate wheat from chaff. Steering error No. 1 for Bollinger is largely uncritical acceptance of V.I. Lenin's imperialism reading of WWI, according to which the world war was above all a conflict among states, each with similar interests and – by implication – not decisively different social structures. In reality the main force – and victorious party – in WWI was no state at all. It was multinational-globalist Anglo-Saxon capital, the two main centres of which were the City of London and Wall Street, but which extended to all the British Commonwealth countries and their colonies and dependencies – in fact all English-speaking settlements worldwide. Although unquestionably capitalist in character, nothing in the global network of Anglo-Saxon capital could be understood without recognizing its specific ethnic quality. Lenin – a British agent trained during no fewer than six sojourns in London[2] to serve as head of state at the eastern end of

---

1 *Die Russen kommen! Wie umgehen mit dem Ukrainekrieg? Über deutsche Hysterie und deren Ursachen.* 2022, Verlag am Park, Berlin. Printed and bound in Poland. Page numbers in parentheses refer to this volume.
2 Lenin's Spring, 1902 London stay featured sustained English language study as well as cultivation of public and private state contacts. In *W.I. Lenin. Biographie*, East Berlin, 1970, p. 127.

the Anglo-Russian secret diplomacy state which had been in service to Anglo-Saxon global capital since the days of George I of Hanover[3] and who (along with his wife) made his living translating Russian documents into English – modified the late 19th century British concept of imperialism to carefully filter out its specifically ethnic English-speaking traits. The message of Lenin's imperialism concept – as discussed in extenso by Bollinger – was that the states of WWI 'imperialism' had about the same interests and character. There was (supposedly) nothing really important to choose between them morally and politically. Besides being false, this assertion contradicted Bollinger's related position that Germany was especially culpable for its conduct in allegedly starting the war, but – never mind.

A second steering error in The Russians are Coming! – clearly related to the first, but nonetheless having plenty of presence in its own right – was Bollinger's decision (so far as his 2022 work went[4]) to systematically ignore the chief source for perspectives on the politics of Wilhelmian Germany and the World War One era– the monumental studies of Max Weber (1865-1920).[5] Probably no one should be allowed to publish work on European history in this period without discussing Weber's contributions – but *Die Russen kommen!* was published anyway. In the 586-odd pages of the Fifth Edition of Weber's collected political writings[6] - which includes excerpts from the sociologist's monographs on the Russian Revolution of 1905 – indispensable insight on the Great War and Germany's role in it is provided. Max Weber intellectual biographer Hinnerk

---

[3] Drischler, The Peace of Utrecht (2022).

[4] Bollinger did cite Weber's political writings in his 2014 tract *Weltbrand, >>Urkatastrophe<< und linke Scheideweg* but quite overlooked Weber's central insight, namely the far-reaching role of bureaucracy over and against capital formations in both Wilhelmian Germany and Czarist Russia.

[5] Wolfgang J. Mommsen noted that ". . . in December 1917 [Weber's] great treatise 'Election Law and Democracy in Germany' [*Wahlrecht und Demokratie in Deutschland*] appeared". In: Mommsen, *Max Weber und die deutsche Politik, 1890-1920*, 1974, p. 291 (Eng. Trans. Michael S, Steinberg, Max Weber and German Politics, 1890-1920, 1984). The editors of The Oxford Handbook of Max Weber (Edith Hanke; Lawrence A. Schaff; and Sam Whimster) (2019) indicated there is no longer any real disputing of the claim Weber was the greatest social scientist to live in the 20th century

[6] *Max Weber. Gesammelte Politische Schriften*, 5th Edition, 1988, Johannes Winckelmann, Ed. Page numbers in brackets refer to this volume. Abbreviated as *GPS*. The 2006 edition of Weber's political writings edited by Daniel Lehmann (*Max Weber. Politik und Gesellschaft*) contains two political articles not included in the *GPS*. The 2919 German-language edition of Weber's political writings (*Max Weber. Kürzere Politische Schriften*)(*KPS*) consists of material culled from the *GPS*. Although most translations provided are original, if a Weber publication quoted appears in the Cambridge Press edition of Weber's political writings (Weber. Political Writings, Peter Lassman and Ronald Speiers, eds., 1994) it will be noted as CW; quotes or excerpts from CW will be treated as ordinary references.

Bruhns[7] indicated in his work on Weber and WWI that some of Weber's insights into the period will probably never be surpassed. Of considerable import in Weber's work is the refutation of Leninist imperialism theory claims that that Czarist Russia wasn't much different from the other "states" participating in WWI. In the 1905-1906 monographs as well as the 1912 Economy and Society outline and his wartime writings also, Weber established beyond peradventure that the Russia of his day was not Western European and hadn't been so since the Tartar Yoke was installed in the 1238-1241 period, even if Western influence was making itself felt. The implication of Weber's analysis was that without comprehension of Russia's non-European cultural background (References 55 and 56 below), neither Russia herself nor the politics of the Triple Entente countries of England and France welded to Russia by 1914 would be understood. Throwing originally Western countries like Germany, France and England into the same pot with Czarist Russia was – Weber indicated – tantamount to giving up on serious historico-political analysis in the era of WWI. What counted in Europe in 1914 was either alignment with Russian despotism (England and France) or opposition to it (actually democratic[8] Germany; Austria-Hungary; Bulgaria).

Between trying to apply the Leninist states-centered imperialism theory (however inconsistently regarding Germany) in a WWI context dominated by the non-state (supra-state) Anglo-Saxon capital alignment; and ignoring the elephant in the living room (Max Weber) regarding the written history of the period, Stefan Bollinger took some of the gloss off his initially plausible 2022 claims that the present day Ukraine-Germany-Russia relation could best be understood by reference to 1905-1920 events in Central and Eastern Europe. Nonetheless said claims retain

---

[7] Hinnerk Bruhns, *Max Weber und der erste Weltkrieg* (2017); see also Drischler, "Max Weber and Russia" (1984), in Max Weber & The Slavs (2019).

[8] Marx insisted that the key criterion for democracy in international affairs was opposition to the Russian despotism of the day; all parties allied with Russian despotism were stigmatized as anti-democratic via 'guilt by association' with Czarism. Formalities such as voting procedures in the various countries counted for little by comparison to Russia alignment, according to Old Moor. For a discussion see Drischler, "Marx and Russia. An Eight-Point Introductory Reconstruction" (1981) in Max Weber & The Slavs (supra, 2019). By Marx's other criterion for democracy – consolidation of a large, unified and sophisticated labor movement (Reference 41 below) – Germany in 1914 was definitely ahead of France and far ahead of England and the other English-speaking countries. Intensity of democratic force (civilizational level) had definite implications for the economic sphere narrowly considered as well. In his path-breaking studies of Polish agricultural workers in the 1890s (the studies which put him on the map as a world-rank social scientist) Max Weber demonstrated that the productivity of Slavic agricultural workers rose steadily when they emigrated into German-speaking areas, i.e., escaped their relative 'culture poverty.'

value, as do other parts of Bollinger's narrative. It might be added that Weber's analysis of the Russia-Germany relation in the 1905-1920 interregnum was not without contradiction. In the 1906 'Pseudo-Constitutionalism' tract, Weber indicated that 'Anglo-Saxon finance capital' was keeping its Russian attack dog at the end of a short tether; but in the "On the Question of 'War Guilt' " contribution of 1919, Czarist Russia alone was blamed for the outbreak of World War I. A genuine attack dog cannot be blamed for anything it does; the master of the canine must bear primary responsibility for its actions.

SECTION ABSTRACT. The First World War was precipitated by hegemony loss anxiety of the Anglo-Saxon capital network grounded in the City of London and Wall Street, a network which dominated the Triple Entente Alliance of England, France and Russia; and had operated the Anglo-Russian secret diplomacy state in tandem with the Russo-Asiatic mode of production in the realm of the Czars since the first part of the 18th century. The network - which was never a state but rather a globalist apparatus - looked upon Germany (and its allies) as a threat to its hegemony across the board. The threat was manifested in the social-democratic and labour movement as embodied in the 2nd International Workingmen's Association and its leader, the Social-Democratic Party of Germany; rapid German scientific development and cultural development in the Wilhelmian Reich, with implications for human species development as a whole; economic, industrial and population growth in Germany which lurched ahead of France and England; and finally, the geo-political positioning of pre-WWI Germany as a potential menace to Anglo-Saxon capital's much-favored attack dog cum gendarme, Czarist Russia. Not one of the chief factors leading to the war represented intentional political warmongering on the part of Germany or its allies. The Leninist imperialism interpretation of the situation – according to which the conflict was one between states – missed the main point, namely that the chief (and prevailing) party in the struggle was no state but a transnational conglomerate which could shift its operating center from the British Isles to North America with consummate ease. Oddly enough, the Leninists and their compatriots seeking to foist responsibility for the war on Germany promptly threw their own method of claiming the 'imperialist' states had about equal culpability out the window when attempting to analyze anything that actually happened circa 1914, this by trying to refer to specifically German traits (or alleged actions). Fortunately the fog bank enveloping these issues can be quickly cut through by use of two key concepts of Max Weber: Anglo-Saxon capital; and hegemony. On this basis of combining these concepts, perceived threats to Anglo-Saxon capital hegemony in 1914 can be identified as the ultimate determinant of the launching of the conflict, and the Central Powers and their populations can be identified as the ultimate (encirclement) victims of Entente aggression, much as the Russian Federation of today (as allied with China) can be identified as the victim of attempted encirclement related to the Ukraine conflict by contemporary Anglo-Saxon capital and *its* allies. Anglo-Saxon global capital is up to its old tricks.

The fourth chapter, "An Antipathy is Born" of Stefan Bollinger's The Russians are Coming! describes German-Russian relations and the overall situation in Europe immediately prior to the unleashing of WWI. Bollinger initially observes that "No one slid into or sleep-walked into this world war, as some of today's historians are again trying to get us to believe"(96). In Reference

No. 111 (227) the 1960s and later controversy concerning Fritz Fischer's work Germany's War Aims in the First World War[9] is discussed.

More an attempted indictment of 1914 Germany than a scholarly work, Fischer's tract came under criticism for, in Bollinger's words, the fact Fischer's effort to identify "the interests which actually guided decisions" was "compromised by over-emphasis on the respective acute occasional considerations and modes of behavior in the crisis" (227). Such amounted to a "conscious attempt to thrust . . . the fundamental political constellation . . . into the background" (ibid) via failure to historically contextualize events in the decades previous to 1914. Intriguingly, such was Max Weber's critique of the efforts of Entente-Allied ideologues to pin a 'war guilt' charge on Germany in 1919. Weber disagreed with the procedures of the German commission seeking to address the war guilt controversy because it accepted – following Wolfgang J. Mommsen[10] - "that the question of responsibility for the war should be virtually entirely confined to consideration of diplomatic actions of the Great Powers in the last weeks and months before the outbreak of the war" and should ignore events of previous years. Weber himself noted in 1919 that "the war alliance [of Russia] with France of 1892, one reaffirmed through the expanded Marine Convention of 1912 [between the two powers] - as well as further alliance measures – were exploited at the appropriate moment to set the 'mechanism of Entente' into motion and ensnare the alliance's friends into the long-premeditated war. This juncture marks the point of the true cause of the origin of the world war."[583]. The Bollinger-Weber consensus that focus on short-run diplomatic manuevers in the weeks and months leading up to the 1914 conflict - such as that conducted by Fritz Fischer - cannot possibly explain the origins of the war is all the more remarkable in that for Weber, the situation constituted definitive proof of the ridiculousness of the Entente-Allied war guilt campaign against Germany, while Bollinger expresses sincere regret the shortcomings of Fischer's polemic lets warmongering Germans off the hook, a group which could readily be convicted of such charges by taking a longer-range perspective (277).

Bollinger then moves on to the heart of his conception of the origins and nature of WWI, namely the Leninist imperialism concept honed during the war, i.e., that the Great Powers England, France, Germany and Russia were all 'imperialist'. Ruefully conceding – for the moment – that the

---

9 Fritz Fischer, Germany's Aims in the First World War (1967)(German original 1961)
10 Wolfgang J. Mommsen, *Max Weber. Zur Neuordnung Deutschlands, Schriften und Reden 1918-1920*, 1991, p. 169.

non-German powers were no better than Germany in this respect, Bollinger states that, despite everything, the war was "an imperialist war which all sides sought, because all sought a new division of the world. This applies to Englishmen and Frenchmen ever so much as Russians." (96). Uniformity of war seeking on the part of the various states could only mean similar motives on the part of the war parties, not to mention similar ultimate socio-political structures. Motives of all the powers, Bollinger claims, were "power, spheres of influence, raw materials, markets, colonies, economic interests in general, and plain and simple Great Power needs."(96). The entire panoply of motivating forces cited by Bollinger appears to mostly reflect Western industrial capitalist practices, not those of the non-Western majority of peoples at the time (for 2000 years China has had a bigger population than all of the European peoples combined). Bollinger then moves on to what he perceives as Germany's special way (*Sonderweg*) into the Great War of 1914, since the notion the Great Powers were about equally culpable for the outbreak contains (for some people) overtones of exculpation of Germany. In addition to all the motives cited above, Germany – following Bollinger – had special needs for a weakened France, a contracted Russia and control of the captive peoples of the Russian Empire, Slav and non-Slav alike (98). Leadership of post-Bismarck Germany – Bollinger claims – fell into the hands of the captains of industry and the banks which grew alongside them, exemplified by August Thyssen and Hugo Stinnes (ibid). The appetite for global expansion of such parties – operating in coalition with the declining but still dangerous great landowner stratum - was allegedly 'insatiable' (*unersaetlich*) (ibid), a clear sign they had arrived at leadership stations. Max Weber's Great Prussian state bureaucracy - which (as will be seen) reportedly controlled nearly everything in Prussianized Germany – makes no appearance in Bollinger's analysis. From Weber's perspective the only possible proof for aggressive expansionism on Wilhelmian Germany's part would be proof the Prussian bureaucracy - running for practical purposes the entire government inclusive of the monarchy – wanted such expansion, which it clearly didn't. Odd expansionistic quotes from industrialists such as those assembled by Bollinger would have very limited probative value, following Weber. What Bollinger would have had to have done to have made his economic analysis[11] of pre-war German politics credible would have been to prove industrialists (or finance

---

[11] In his 2014 treatment of WWI causes (Ref. 4 above) Bollinger goes so far as to state :"Without [clarification of] economic interests, no analysis of causes of war [is possible] (p. 53). As Mommsen observes (Mommsen, 1974, p. 258), Weber viewed economic causation as secondary in 1914.

capitalists) (or their agents) were truly at the helm of state, something Bollinger simply assumes, not proves. Recent history shows clearly enough that *nouveau riche* elements have had problems translating their newfound wealth into functioning political power networks; there is no reason to assume the *nouveau riche* German industrialists of the 1880s and 1890s were any different. Weber also observes that the Russian *nouveau riche* at the time (in addition to the German) were politically ineffectual ([257]; Weber 2006, p. 306; *KPS* p. 135; CW). Translating newly-acquired capital into political influence can be a complicated business, not a push-button operation as Bollinger seems to suggest.

For those with a taste for accentuated disagreement in political analysis, the controversy between Bollinger and Max Weber concerning alleged Wilhelmian German aggressiveness is apposite. In Karl Palonen's far-reaching article in The Oxford Handbook of Max Weber,[12] it was observed that [in 1895] "Weber blames Germans for Germany's late and timid engagement in power politics overseas . . . Without participating in the competition for colonies, Germany could not maintain its status as one of the Great Powers . . ."(ibid). Germans' psycho-social tendency regarding external politics in general and colonial matters also to assume a 'wimpardly' (*schlüchtern*) ([21]; Weber 2006, p. 59; *KPS* p. 19; CW), non-aggressive posture endangers overall national development, the sociologist Weber warns. "At first quite tardily, wimpardly and half-heartedly Germans began an overseas 'power politics' which wasn't even worthy of the name" (ibid). He adds that "The *most threatening aspect* of our situation . . . is that the bourgeois classes appear too withered on the vine (*verwelken*) to serve as vehicles of the *power* interests of the nation . . ." ([23]; Weber 2006, p. 61; *KPS* p. 22; CW). Germans' lack of aggressive instincts and power politics drive, Weber concludes, means that the shortfall of "*political* qualifications of the *ruling and ascendant classes* constitutes the ultimate *socio*-political problem of the nation"[ibid]. German politicians of the day (1895), Weber goes on to note, display "no trace of national passion – they lack the great *power* instincts of a class capable of exercising [authentic] political leadership" ([22]; Weber 2006, p. 60; *KPS* p. 21; CW). In his 1898 contribution to a survey concerning expansion of the German fleet, Weber lamented the lack of will for Germany to engage in "overseas expansion," the failure to marshal the "missing strength and courage" ([31]; Weber 2006, p. 68) regarding naval affairs which would be required to make Germany a genuine

---

12 Karl Palonen, "The Supranational Dimension in Max Weber's Vision of Politics," in E. Hanke, et al., 2019, pp. 261; 273.

participant in world commerce. As Mommsen noted (Mommsen, 1974, p. 148), Bismarck's cringing lack of will to pursue consistent colonialism was a source of irritation for Weber.

In contrast – to say the least – Bollinger, in both The Russians are Coming! work and the volume World Conflagration, 'Fundamental Catastrophe' and the Parting of Ways of the Left[13] claims there was no parallel in the civilized world to the aggressive instincts and externally expansionist state policy of Germans in the decades leading up to 1914. If these contentions were true, they would drive a coach and twelve through the German political scientist's claim reviewed above that all the imperialist states of 1914 were about equally culpable for the outbreak and conduct of the war, but consistency is not always available.

In The Russians are Coming! Bollinger identified two groups of explanations for supposed German aggression in the run-up to WWI. The first group would be imperialist power drives and motives common to all the war parties as described above, e.g., power, raw materials, markets, new colonies, economic interests in general and so on, and above all the effort to secure a new division of the globe. The second group – drives specific to Germany – was seen as including perceived needs for a weakened France, subservient Belgium, contracted Russia and the transformation of formerly captive Russian nationalities – e.g., Finns and Ukrainians – into independent entities which could permanently buffer the Russian Empire. But there were additional, special reasons for German aggression in the period, Bollinger maintains. Although all the Great Powers seemed to be seeking a new division of the planet, for German purposes "The world seemed [already] divided" (101). Most of what was readily susceptible to European colonization had already been seized prior to German unification in 1871. For this reason German power projection would have to reach out in all directions at once to obtain anything worthwhile – unlike any other of the principal parties to WWI. In the 2014 Conflagration work Bollinger pointed to yet another special factor supposedly consolidating aggressive policy preferences in Germany, namely "The peculiar manner in which state military initiative, economic competence and cleverness were welded together"(*verschmolzen*).[14] Typical here – the argument went on to say – was the development of the Zeppelin. In this respect, it was observed, "it was above all the indefatigable, recently privatized General von Zeppelin who was to thank for the zeppelin craze. Sympathy, cash and much greater money transfers flowed to him for his research and construction

---

13 Bollinger, 2014
14 Ibid, p. 39.

activities, activities planned from the start as militarily grounded" (ibid). Bollinger's observations in this respect could be seen as an embryonic military-industrial complex theory. What counts for evaluating the German political scientist's overall model of Germany's pre-war political and social structure is in any case how it compares to the alternative Weber-derived Anglo-Saxon capital world hegemony model[15] mentioned earlier. Prior to developing the latter in more detail, a preliminary review of Bollinger's contentions is in order.

PRELIMINARY REVIEW OF BOLLINGER AND THE OUTBREAK OF THE GREATWAR. As mentioned in the section summary above, the four leading factors precipitating the attack upon the Central Powers in 1914 (actually - at the military level - an attack on ascendant German-led Continental Europe conducted by peripheral powers) in line with the Anglo-Saxon capital world hegemony perspective, were:

- Threat of the German social-democratic and labour movement and its 2nd International affiliates to Anglo-Saxon (and all other) capitalist groupings;
- Rapid German scientific and cultural development in the 1880s and after, with implications for human species development as a whole;
- Economic, industrial and population growth outstripping the other European nations; and
- Geo-political positioning of Germany as a threat to Russia.

It's important to bear in mind that these four variables represent a Weber-derived reconstruction of medium and long run factors conditioning the attack of 1914 - not Weber's overt statements concerning the short-run precipitant of the outbreak of hostilities. The only major short-run factor precipitating outbreak of hostilities for Weber was Russian imperialism – nothing else, even if the sociologist at the same time insisted that serious evaluation of ultimate war responsibility claims could never be based solely on review of short-run events. Also, the German sociologist would never have agreed that the SPD and the 2nd International represented a serious threat to German or world capital. After attending an SPD convention in Mannheim in 1906 and several party meetings, Weber concluded the pre-war social-democrats were a "harmless" (Mommsen, 1974, p.

---

[15] A. Gramsci was being ethnically specific when he wrote of 'Anglo-Saxon world hegemony.' In: Stefan Bollinger and Juha Koivisto, "Hegemonic Apparatus," in Historical Materialism 17 (2009).

114) labour lobby, not a movement whose leaders had "power instincts." In this respect Bollinger's position in The Russians are Coming! that the pre-war German labour movement represented a real potential threat to global capital is likely preferable to that of Weber. Reference 49 to follow provides some hard numbers on the vastly greater size of the pre-war German social democracy vis-á-vis, for example, French socialists, this size difference a completely unsurprising reason for capitalists to plot war against Germany.

The next consideration is how to conduct preliminary evaluation of the competing interpretations. This is simpler than one might expect. The provisional question is: do the aspects highlighted by Bollinger outweigh the four variables listed above to the point of tipping the scales in favor of the judgment that Germany and its allies ignited WWI for – in current terms - unacceptable reasons? Or – put negatively – what are the limitations of Bollinger's perspective? The chief limitation of Bollinger's approach is that it is sufficiently Leninism-influenced to constitute a de-centered totality. This means it doesn't hold together. For any version of the Leninist imperialism theory to hold, the chief combatants of WWI would have had to have similar status of being states. But – as was claimed earlier – the most important party to the conflict was no state but rather a capitalist emanation of the English-speaking peoples, the Anglo-Saxon capital global hegemony structure. It was larger and more powerful than any state, was hegemonic for centuries in Europe - and by the Victorian Era over the planet - and perceived its broad and long-term interests in a more cosmopolitan manner than ordinary elected officials. Between more resources and broader perspectives than most office holders, *it* decided on where and when Western states would be involved in major hostilities. Neither Germany nor German-led ascendant Continental Europe had enough wherewithal in 1914 to subdue the dragon, even it they did have the means to threaten its hegemony. A further plausibility constraint on the contention of Bollinger that the major combatants in the Great War had similar imperialist goals was the utter institutional peculiarity of the Czarist orientally despotic/Chinggisid regime, which Weber indicated in his Economy and Society work was more Chinese than European (See Reference 22 to follow).

Bollinger's other two key theses – that the outbreak of WWI can only be understood in decades-long historical context, and that the titanic nature of the 1914-1919 conflict provides useful material for comparison with today's events such as the conflict in Ukraine – retain plausibility.

Before comparing the Anglo-Saxon capital hegemony network's encirclement of Germany in 1914 and its encirclement of Russia today however more detailed examination of Max Weber's concept of state and politics is called for. No single theorist of politics today has excelled the German's overall framework for international political analysis, even though all his material is now more than a century old.

II. Max Weber's Model of Germany in the Era of the Great War, 1914-1919

The Introduction to the Cambridge Press edition of Weber's political writings[16] has several useful observations on Weber's political thought in relation to other currents in modern political studies. Weber's concept of democracy (" . . .'democracy' is never an end in itself . . . "(Weber, 2006. p. 50)) is especially distinctive, since it can mean massification, bureaucratization or instrumental mobilization for state tasks (i.e., increasing war morale), as well as the ordinary meaning today of increasing mass participation in public affairs for public benefit – the latter above all taking the form of the struggle to increase voting rights for and political participation by returning war veterans via universal manhood suffrage. Particularly in the 1918 article dealing with Parliament and Government in Newly Ordered Germany ([308]; Weber 2006, p. 350;) but also the 1917 article "An Emergency Election Law for the Reich" ([192]; Weber, 2006, p. 240) the sociologist's zeal for expanded voting rights for veterans came into relief. In the former contribution Weber observed that "Democratization of election law . . . is an urgent and politically unavoidable task of the hour . . . "([406]; Weber 2006, p. 431; CW).

But the Cambridge Press Introduction to Weber's political writings is diffuse, so to speak. It does not grasp the degree to which Weber's political thought is Russo-centric[17] and which operates -

---

16 CW, pp. vii to xxv
17 For a comparison of Marx's Russo-centric political theory and Weber's Russo-centric political theory, see Drischler 2019. Both agreed that Russia had a non-Western political heritage and was unlikely to transform herself without intervention from the West (inclusive of hostile military intervention, above all from Germany). But Weber – no Russophobe – was convinced that cumulative Western influence could eventually lead to democratic consolidation in Russia and displayed real sympathy for the Russian people. Marx's approach by contrast was to seek to overthrow the Russia state come what may, and if the Russian nation disappeared in the process, it would have been no particular loss for him. Marx's enthusiasm for the German social-democrats' war credits vote in August, 1914 would have been unbounded. Bollinger describes the Marxist pedigree of the 1914 German social-democrats' attitude toward Russia (104), this with reference to the work of Karl A. Wittfogel (228). See also the Appendix ("Oriental Despotism and August 1914") below.

regarding the Wilhelmian state – with a bi-polar scheme of Russia-similar bad/England-similar good. This state of affairs is illustrated by the chart on the following page. Broadly speaking, the state traits tending toward the left side of the chart (Russia) are empirical-pernicious (acutally present and negative), while moving toward the right (British constitutionalism) one encounters mostly non-existent positive-normative goals, as opposed to descriptions of Prusso-German institutional practices. The pernicious domestic tendencies at the top of the chart endanger national unity, thereby endangering state operations internationally. Russia-similar with regard to the Wilhelmian state does not, as a rule, necessarily mean Russia-influenced or bespeak Russian infiltration for Weber. Although Weber wrote of Russian-sponsored peasant infiltration ([7]; Weber 2006 p. 8; *KPS* p. 8; CW) of Polish and Russian seasonal agricultural labourers into eastern Germany operating at a sub-German cultural level - both with regard to literacy and production energy as well as life-style practices - when describing Wilhelmian political structures as Russia-similar, Weber is using a generally perjorative designation for phenomena which – even if evincing some parallels with Russian modes of operation – do not necessarily represent actual Russian transplants or outgrowths. Complicating matters somewhat is that in the course of peppering his major writings with perjorative Russia-similar references, Weber – as was his right as a recognized Russia specialist and devotee of comparative approaches to politics– makes reference to actual acts of the Russian state. Of course for Weber's own evaluation purposes, stakes in differentiating the two types of statements were likely modest, but clarification of the general practice is not without use. In short, Weber's political thought is Russia-informed even when the ostensible topic is not Russia.

In the following, review of some of Weber's Russia-related observations will be undertaken to provide overview before dealing with one of Weber's key innovations in political theory, an innovation which was especially evident in the Russia monographs of 1905-1906 and also mentioned in the Introduction to the Cambridge Press edition of the political writings. This contention was that the liberal-individualist values of Western civilization had been consolidated as a values bedrock before liberalism's economic form, industrial capitalism, took definitive shape in the specific 19th-century Western context, and by 1905 evidence had mounted that the 19th-century linking of Western values, industrialization and human emancipation was a one-time affair, this signaling that Russia (and other countries) could move forward with industrialization

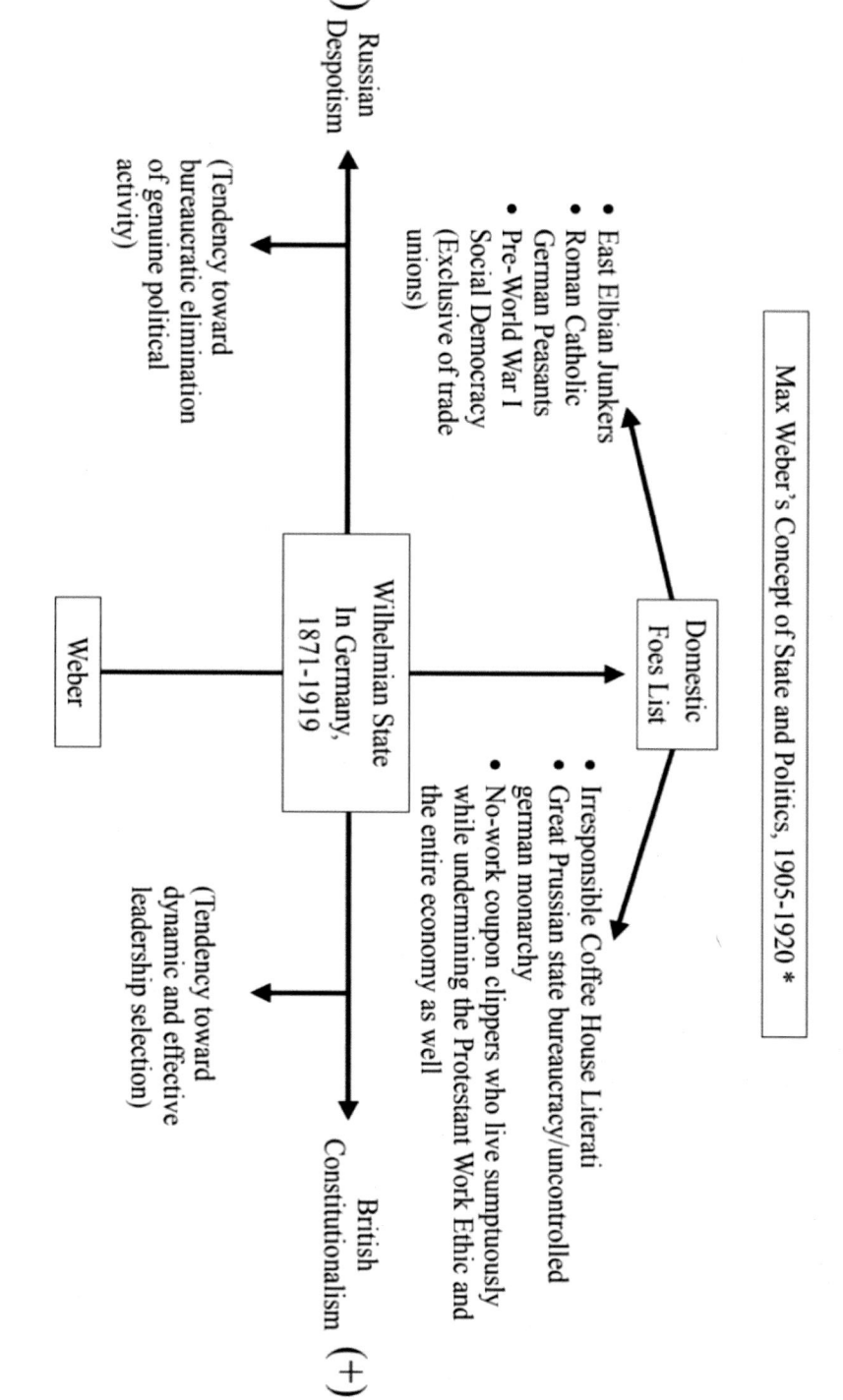

Max Weber's Concept of State and Politics, 1905-1920 *

Wilhelmian State In Germany, 1871-1919

Weber

Domestic Foes List:
- East Elbian Junkers
- Roman Catholic German Peasants
- Pre-World War I Social Democracy (Exclusive of trade unions)
- Irresponsible Coffee House Literati
- Great Prussian state bureaucracy/uncontrolled german monarchy
- No-work coupon clippers who live sumptuously while undermining the Protestant Work Ethic and the entire economy as well

Russian Despotism (−) ← (Tendency toward bureaucratic elimination of genuine political activity)

British Constitutionalism (+) ← (Tendency toward dynamic and effective leadership selection)

* As developed in Weber *GPS* (1988) and Drischler, *Max Weber & The Slavs* (2019)

or even tendential capitalizaton without any major emancipatory effects on the populace as a whole. On this basis, an exposition of Weber's many-sided portrayl of Russian aggression in the approach to WWI will be undertaken. After the Anglo-Saxon capital global hegemony network's 1914 Russian attack dog has been described, the network itself may be further depicted, synthesizing (as Weber did not) the German sociologist's notions of hegemony and ethnically specific capital formation. It will then be seen that not only is the 1914 encirclement tactic against Germany being repeated today against the Russian Federation in Ukraine, but the very same social group - Anglo-Saxon capital – is doing the encircling. And this for the very same reason – quite reasonably perceived threats to its global hegemony.

a. Russia-Prussia Analogies, following Weber

Weber begins the description of his his pseudo-parliamentarism concept by developing the related pseudo-constitutionalism (fake constitutionalism) concept in the 1905 tract "On the State of Bourgeois Democracy in Russia." Discussing the prospect of the liberalization which would constitute the essential precondition to achieving Western-style parliamentarism or constitutionalism in the wake of the 1905 Revolution, Weber observes that "motives in favor of a liberal policy carry, of course, only limited weight with [Count Sergei] Witte, let alone with the Czar and his entourage. The question is only: What degree of stress will they withstand, before the temptation to resort to a military dictatorship as a preliminary to some kind of fake constitutionalism (*Scheinkonstitutionalismus*) becomes too strong to resist? Such an outcome is of course well within the bounds of possibility in the near future"(Wells and Baehr, p. 103; [56]; Weber 2006 p. 111; CW). In his 1906 follow-up tract to On the State of Bourgeois Democracy in Russia, that is, "Russia's Transition to Pseudo-Constitutionalism" as well as discussions of the Russian Duma leading up to his definitive analysis of pseudo-parliamentarism in the "Parliament and Government in Reordered Germany" contribution of 1916, Weber denounced the "swindle" of the Duma in the respect that both the Czar and his entourage were determined to present just enough of a facade of parliamentarism as to block criticism of Russian anti-democracy in the Entente countries such as France and England (and soon the USA) while reassuring both Anglo-Saxon and French bankers propping up the Russian regime that their investments would be protected ever so much as their counsel on state affairs would continue to be respected, above all (in 1916) continuing the war effort. After making reference to criticisms of his own work by future Russian premier Kerensky ([337, Ref. 1]; Weber 2006 p. 263); CW) and related Russian matters, Weber steps forward to present his prime example of pseudo-parliamentarism but – *Quelle suprendre!* - it's Prussia, not Russia. Weber writes ([363]; Weber 2006 p. 396; CW) that "Alternatives to *conservative* provincial legislatures are impossible in Prussia, and German pseudo-parliamentarism (*Scheinparlamentarismus*) rests in all its implications upon the extant (since 1878), from party interests maintained axiom that every regime and its proponents must by natural necessity be 'conservative'. . . . This and absolutely nothing else is what 'non-partisanship' means in our system of bureauratic rule. . . The party interests of the conservative bureaucracy currently in power - as well as the interest group circles subordinated to it - control political direction of the country all by themselves". The ease with which Weber moves back and forth between Russia and Prussia-Germany when describing bureaucratic domination of society is arresting, and it is clear Weber's immersion in Russia studies 1905-1906 colored his work thereafter.[18] Thus in the article "The Prussian Election Law" of April 1917 (Weber 2006, p. 250) the sociologist warns of a Russian trick to sidetrack universal suffrage reform in Germany, stating "As in Russia, they [opponents of universal manhood suffrage] will seek to retain their power via a phoney 'democratization' to be obtained by tossing bits and pieces of democracy to certain sectors of petty landholders." Wells and Baehr (Wells and Baehr, pp. 19-20) however caution about over-stressing Russia-Prussia convergence in Weber's political analysis, writing " . . . Russian autocratic power and domestic coercion was far more severe than that exercised by its western neighbor. It is true that Weber often used his Russian essays to attack, directly or through allusion, Bismarck's legacy and the 'personal rule' of Wilhelm II . . . . Nonetheless, he was clear where such comparisons ended. Even the most basic political and civil liberties were still to be achieved in Russia, as was a functioning parliament. The German Reichstag may have stood condemned, as Weber later expressed it, as the bearer of 'negative politics' . . . . But at least Germany in 1905 *had* an established parliament, and with it political parties which to a considerable degree could openly and legally mobilize for social and political reform." Weber's unconditional support for the 1914 War Credits vote in the Reichstag and the initial German war effort in WWI – like that of the majority social-democrats – could only be based on

---

[18] The most influential discussion of Weber's proclivity to move from Prussia to Russia and back in critical political analysis remains that of Wolfgang J. Mommsen (Mommsen, 1974, pp. 154-155).

the belief that, despite some analogies between Wilhelmian Germany and Czarist Russia, Russia was qualitatively more anti-democratic than Germany and the Central Powers, and English and French support for Czarism in 1914 compromised the claims to defend progressive values advanced by both countries. Though Weber may at times have judged the Wilhelmian German system harshly, he never went so far as to say it was as regressive as the Czarist system of the day, this latter the – utterly dubious – claim of the Entente powers in 1914. (See Map 1.) Weber's contention of long-term French 'vassalage' to Russia ([118]; Weber 2006, p. 169) - including the war provocative extension of military service in France to three years to appease the Czar and the Russia-aping pseudo-parliament of Napoleon III ([287]; Weber 2006 p. 332; KPS p. 162)[19] - meant categorical rejection of French claims to moral leadership at the outset of WWI on the part of the German sociologist. The unreformable Anglophile Weber would never have written something so unflattering about the British however.

b. Weber on the Historical Specificity
of the Rise of Western Liberalism and
it's Inapplicability to 20th Century Russia

In their "Editors' Introduction" to The Russian Revolutions. Max Weber,[20] Gordon C. Wells and Peter Baehr observed that so far as Weber's Russia perspective went, "among the chief impediments to liberal democracy . . . [was] the relatively late industrialization experienced by . . Russia . . . . During capitalism's nascent phrase, Weber explains, material interests and individualistic ethos has tended to coincide . . . . In Russia . . . in contrast, this developmental stage had been missed and, consequently, individualism now found itself 'swimming against the tide' of material constellations . . . . Re-emphasizing this point, Weber added that, in Russia, all 'those intermediate stages are missing, which in the West placed the powerful *economic* interests

---

19 For confirmation of Weber's contention French Emperor Napoleon III was Russo-dependent, see William F. Drischler, "Marx's Best Polemic: Russo-Napoleonism and the Italian Question in *Herr Vogt, Beiträge zur Marx-Engels-Forschung. Neue Folge* [*BzMEF.NF*], 1994; William F. Drischler, "Bismarck – Russian Agent in the Tartar Troika. Marx on the Rise of the Iron Chancellor," *BzMEF.NF*, 1997; and William F. Drischler, "Louis-Napoleon as Russo-Asiatic Agent. Marx's Revision of *The 18th Brumaire* in *Herr Vogt*," *BzMEF.NF,* 1998. Louis Napoleon's practice of rule via street gangs was Russian through-and-through, according to Weber. The French emperor's de facto stepfather was the Russian Czar. See also the treatment of Raymond Poincaré in the Excursus to follow.

20 Wells and Baehr, 1997, pp. 17-18

of propertied strata in the service of the bourgeois freedom movement'. . . . A second obstacle to the establishment of liberal democracy common to both Germany and Russia was the subordinate political position of the 'bourgeoisie' itself. Heavy industry, big manufacture, finance capital, wealthy commercial interests, far from achieving political power, had largely capitulated to the . . state."

Weber's historicist point – as mentioned earlier – was that the constellation of liberal-individualistic ethos and industrial capitalist development in latter 19th-century Europe (this conditioned in part by religious beliefs that had long since given way to secularization) was not only unprecedented, but also likely unrepeatable anywhere in the modern, 20th-century world. In On the State of Bourgeois Democracy in Russia Weber observed that "the struggle for . . . 'individualistic' values must take account of the 'material' condition of the environment at every step, the realization of these values must not be left to 'economic development'. 'Democracy' and 'individualism' would stand little chance today if we were to rely for their 'development' on the 'automatic' effect of *material* interests" (Wells and Baehr, p. 108; [63]; Max Weber 2006, pp. 116-117; CW). He adds that "The historical development of modern 'freedom' had as its presupposition a peculiar and ne'er to be repeated constellation of factors. Let us enumerate the most important of these. Firstly, overseas expansion . . . Secondly the specificity of the economic and social structure of the 'early capitalist' epoch in Western Europe and thirdly the conquest of life through science, the process of coming-to-itself of the spirit (*Zusichselbstkommen des Geistes*) . . . Finally: certain value conceptions growing out of the concrete historical specificity of a definite religious thought world which, in conjunction with utterly unique political factors and with the material preconditions mentioned above, shaped the 'ethical' specificity and 'cultural values' of modern man" (Translated in Drischler, Max Weber & The Slavs, Part I, p.13-14; [64-65]; alternative translation in Wells and Baehr, p.109; Max Weber 2006, pp. 117; CW). Weber concludes that "The question of whether any material development, let alone today's high capitalist development, could preserve these unique historical conditions, let alone create new ones, needs only to be put for the answer to be obvious" (Wells and Baehr, ibid; [65]; Max Weber 2006, p. 118; CW).

The upshot of Weber's pronounced historicism in political analysis was that so far as curbing Russian aggression in the post-1905 context went, only outside military intervention or quasivoluntaristic action inside Russia could move the czarist regime in a pro-democratic and peaceful direction and away from the consolidating Triple Entente alliance against Germany and Austria-Hungary. Such was the last thing foreign financiers (Read: the Anglo-Saxon capital global hegemony network) wanted, Weber suggested, but he refused to rule out the possibility that cumulative exposure to Western cultural influence (short of war) might help precipitate meaningful internal change in Russia. This differed from Marx's "Who's shooting at the Russians? Let's join them" basic attitude[21] toward the realm of the Czars.

c. Weber's Thesis of incomparable Imperialism and Aggressiveness of Russia as a determinative factor of the outbreak of WWI

Delineation of the historic specificity of the development of Western individualist values and the general non-applicability of the European sequence to post-1905 Russia was important to coming to an understanding of Weber's overall political project, this because it helped the set the stage for both the characterization of Russian imperialism as unique *and* the identification of said imperialism as a determinative factor of the outbreak of WWI.
In the "Between Two Laws" newspaper article of February 1916 Weber observed that "The mere existence of a Great Power, as we [Germans] have become, constitutes a road block to other power states, above all: [the Russian state] buffeted between the cultural deprivation (*Kulturmangel*) of the Russian peasants and the power interests of the Russian state church and bureaucracy. There is no means in sight by which this [situation] could have been changed" ([143-144]; Max Weber 2006, p. 191; *KPS* p. 59-60; CW) . . . .If there is no way to divert the Russian expansion drive (*Expansionsdrang*) in a direction away from us . . . it will remain in the future (ibid)." As an authority on agrarian production and peasant politics, Weber returned to the agrarian side of Russian aggression in the article "Germany under the European World Powers" of October, 1916, writing that ". . . regarding our position vis-à-vis Russia one finds an economic element which is completely absent from the Western powers: Russian people's imperialism (*Volksimperialismus*) as an Austrian social-democrat calls it – the expansion tendency caused by

---

21 Drischler, "Marx and Russia, etc.", 2019. Marx's Turkophilia (supporting Turkey against Russia in every 19th-century military conflict) stems from his attitude on the Russian question.

the land hunger of the Russian peasants. This is a product of a [backward] cultural state which will eventually recede; but in the short run, it will get worse" ([164]; Max Weber 2006, p. 217; *KPS* p. 69). Both cause and effect of people's imperialism, Weber contended, was adherence to "archaic national peasant ideals" of the agricultural workforce ([125]; *KPS* p. 43). Although disinclined to develop a narrowly economic framework for explaining Russia aggression, Weber did concede that the goals of Russian agrarian elements included "the sacrifice (*Opfer*) of our [central European] agricultural system" ([163]; Max Weber 2006 p. 216; *KPS* p. 68). In the same article Weber wrote that "Regarding Russia, the real, that is, the political grounds for the war, were on the one hand the power interests of the bureaucracy and the grand dukes [Russian: 'serving men' – WFD]. On the other side was the *Pan-slavist legend* "([168]; Max Weber 2006 p.220; *KPS* p. 72). This latter factor Weber attributes to the activities of Russia's Teutopohobic pseudo-intelligentsia which aligned with the Russian war effort in 1914. The possibility of "the Russian bureaucracy [achieving] domination over all Slavs"(ibid) was seen as partially dependent upon the intelligentsia beating the drums for such a project, following Weber.

And so a preliminary list of factors fueling Russian aggression en route to precipitating WWI from Weber's purview would include:

- peasant people's imperialism;
- Russian agrarian production competition with Germany and its allies;
- power interests of the bureaucracy;
- power interests of the state church;
- power interests of the grand dukes; and
- interest of the intelligentsia in consolidating its position via advocacy of Pan-slavism.

Weber also makes reference to the interests of urban Russian munitions workers in encouraging a war-like state policy, but this group would not have been of the impact of the major players. A Bolshevik innovation of 1918, Weber also wrote, was Russian "soldiers' imperialism" ([293]; Max Weber 2006 p. 338; *KPS* p. 168) which threatened every state bordering Russia.

It's worthy of note most of the pre-1914 interests outlined by Weber are not even mentioned in the effort of Stefan Bollinger in The Russians are Coming! to outline common – for the most part economic – factors allegedly motivating all the Great Powers at the outbreak of war. The Russian

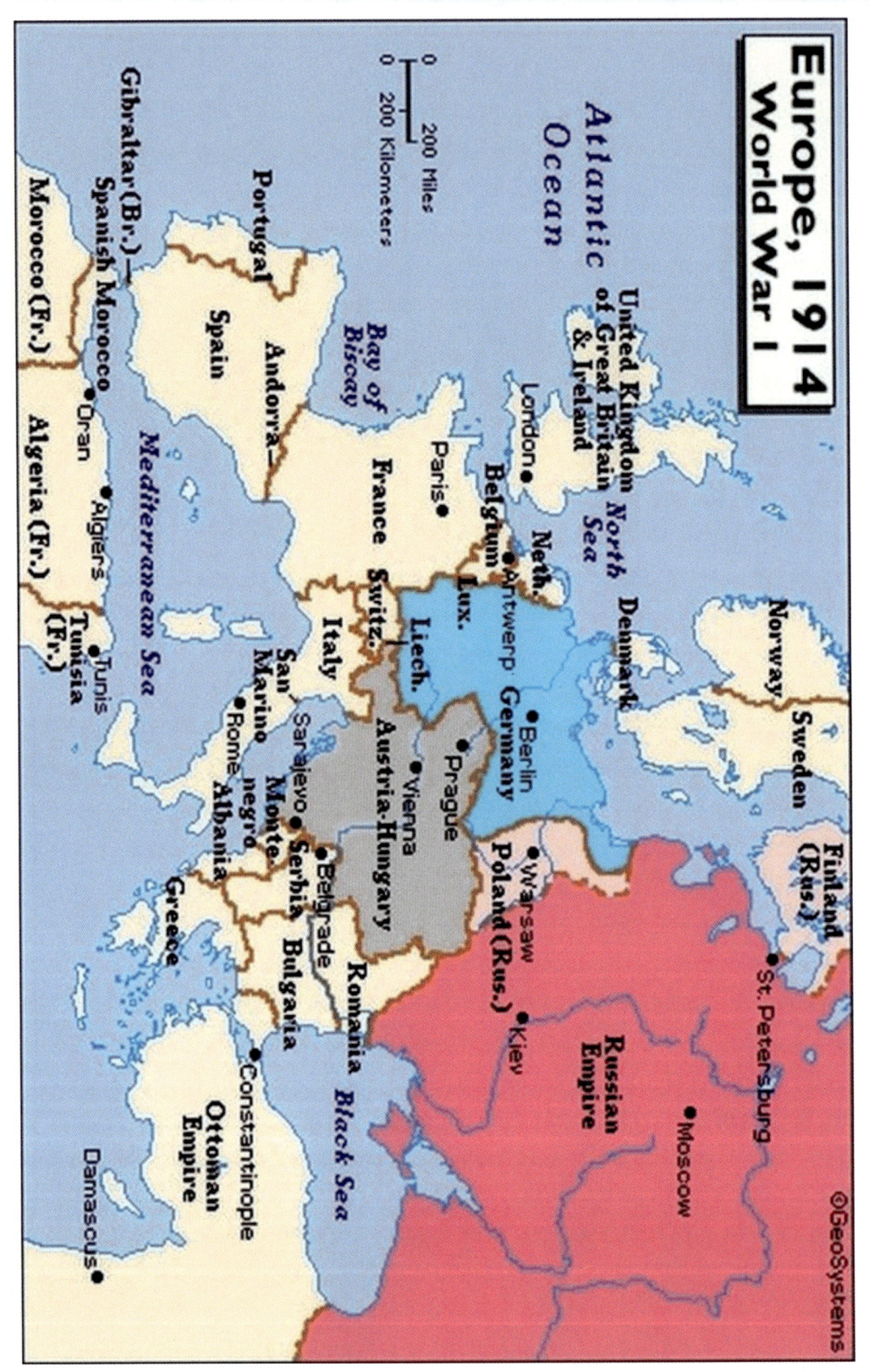

Map 1 Europe in August, 1914

state and social structure varied widely from that of the West, particularly with regard to the huge peasant majority and overweening state bureaucracy, both – according to the Weber of the Economy and Society mostly written in 1912[22] – displaying numerous archaic Chinese (Sino-Mongol) traits as opposed to anything European. The net effect of this unique pro-war constellation in any case, the exposition continues, was that "The threat issuing from *Russia* was the only one [among the belligerent states] that directed itself *against our existence* as a national power state overall . . . Russia threatens not merely the status of our state, but rather our entire culture, and above and beyond that the culture of the whole world, *so long* as it is structured as it is now. These considerations apply to no other power "([169];Max Weber 2006, pp. 220-221; *KPS* p. 73). Weber concluded by writing "In the Russia of 1914 there was no social stratum of any sort of positive influence which would *not* have wanted war" ([491]; Weber 2006, p. 527; *KPS* p. 228), this no surprise since the German sociologist had long claimed Russian militarism was the one of the worst in history (and was later to claim Russia's 1919 militarism was the worst "present anywhere at this time" ([293]; Max Weber 2006 p 338; *KPS* p. 168 (See excursus.)).

Such is an outline of Weber's contention of unique aggression drives ("police absolutism") ([106]; Weber, 2006, p.152; CW) in Russia in the run-up to August 1914. The Russian tactic of igniting world war in 1914 was part and parcel of far broader strategic concerns of a non-state network, the Anglo-Saxon capital global hegemony group. Though little understood, the group can be clearly identified using two ideas of Weber – hegemony and Anglo-Saxon capital (or Anglo-Saxon finance capital). Once identified, the network can be readily seen to be sponsoring military conflict in Ukraine today for the same reason it did in Europe in 1914 – hegemony loss anxiety.

d. The Anglo-Saxon Capital
World Hegemony Network -
A Weberian Reconstruction

---

[22] Drischler, 2022. Ayşe Zarakol has described Czarist Russia as Chinggisid, i.e. combining Chinese bureaucratism with Mongol aggressiveness, this combination originating in the Yuan Mongol conquest dynasty in 13th century China and then spreading throughout Asia, but developing a particularly pure form – according to Zarakol - during the Tartar Yoke in Russia, 1241-1480. Thus Russian aggression against Germany in 1914 had important roots in the actions of illiterate 13th century Mongol animist horsemen who had no choice but to retain Chinese bureaucrats in order to administer their empire. In The Russians are Coming! Bollinger has very little to say about the Czarist social structure, the structure Weber maintains was axiologically determinative for the entire course of events.

i *Hegemony*. As indicated in Reference 15 above, Antonio Gramsci (1891-1937) stole a march on the project of synthesizing Weber's hegemony and Anglo-Saxon capital concepts by describing "Anglo-Saxon world hegemony." Hegemony is usually taken to denote predominance of an apparatus by a combination of consent and acquiescence, and often is taken to suggest remote ideological and other control of the dominated group by apparatus operators. Weber's hegemony ideas are focused on the Prussian bureaucracy's role in Wilhelmian Germany as a whole, the sociologist having spent the better part of a decade in and around the Prussian legal bureaucracy. The key texts *re* hegemony are "Parliament and Government in Newly Ordered Germany" of May 1918 and "Germany's Future State Form" of November-December 1918. In the passage quoted above from the May 1918 contribution wherein Weber advocated democratization, he goes on – in his customary fashion of never advocating democracy without giving a utilitarian or reason-of-state grounds to advocate it – to touch upon hegemony. He writes "The democratization of *election law* . . . is an urgent and politically unavoidable task of the hour, above all for the German hegemony state ([406]; Weber 2006 p. 431; CW). Weber is here speaking of the proposed abolition of the Prussian three-tier voting system, which – if retained until the soldiers returned home from the war – would have allowed those who stayed out of combat and enriched themselves at the expense of those in the trenches (to use another WWI expression) to oppress the latter upon their return. If such oppression occurred, Weber went on to argue, the resulting bitterness of the veterans would thoroughly de-legitimate the German government. Under these conditions a truly functional – i.e., hegemonic - state would not be possible. And so this version of hegemony following Weber primarily refers to functionality of the state entity, not predominance of a state apparatus over masses of ideologically conformed subjects.

Weber's second reference to hegemony in the the Parliament and Government in Newly Ordered Germany piece of 1918 also refers to state functionality, in this instance regarding budget law and procedure in the Reichstag. He writes ([414-415]; Weber 2006, p. 438; CW): "The budget law of the Reichstag forces the Reichskanzler – not only as a reich minister but also [in the capacity of serving] as the bearer of the presiding parliamentary voice and proponent of the hegemony state (*Hegemoniestaats*) – to answer to the Reichstag." [23] Once again hegemony is more the

---

23 CW translates this passage as follows. "The right of the Reichstag to approve the budget forces the Reichskanzler, not only as a minister of the Reich but also as the holder of the presidial vote in the Bundesrat and representative of the hegemonial state [to answer] for the conduct of Reich policy as it is influenced by Prussia, which means in practice having to face up to questioning" (pp. 241-242).

embodiment of undivided sovereignty than elite domination of the masses for Weber, even if the hegemonic state unquestionably rules from the top down.

Weber's third set of references to hegemony in the May 1918 tract are closer to contemporary hegemony thinking in that they refer to the outcome of a domination struggle, one marked by competition of clearly juxtaposed parties. Ostensibly the struggle is between the federal Reich bureaucracy supposedly under the direction of the Reichstag and the Prussian provincial bureaucracy, supposedly under the direction of the provincial legislature (*Landtag*). The two bureaucracies – the 'Great Prussian' federal bureaucracy and the provincial bureaucracy - mutually influence one another regarding both personnel patronage plums and actual governmental policy, Weber claims in his strikingly modern narrative, this based on their common interest in avoiding legislative scrutiny and control of their various misdemeanors. So the first meaning of 'hegemony' here is the Prussian federal bureacracy's particular reach – as an interest group – for obtaining (or reinforcing) apparatus control over the German government as a whole, what could be termed special hegemony. The second aspect of hegemony is the overall character of the hegemony state (*Hegemoniestaat*)([417]; Max Weber 2006 p. 440; CW) or general rule in the country in light of Prussian 'Reich hegemony policy' as it has come to be consolidated. What the Great Prussian bureaucracy has done, it is suggested, is to parlay its winnings in struggle with the Reichstag to aid the Prussian provincial bureaucracy in its struggles with the provincial *Landtag*, this on condition that the latter doesn't interfere with national policy direction as a whole on the part of the former. Special and general hegemony merge into - simple hegemony. Weber writes (ibid): "The result of the previous considerations is this: the internal policy of Prussia remains unaffected by the reich [reich authorities] insofar as consideration of major affairs of state do not compel another course. Within the context of reich hegemony policy (*Reichshegemoniepolitik*) one finds a mutual influencing of [on the one hand] a reichstag-influenced bureaucratic directive apparatus and [on the other hand] a *Landtag*-influenced provincial government directive apparatus, said structures dealing with personnel as well as objective governmental aspects." Weber goes on to summarize by stating (ibid): "Depending upon whether the governmental instances controlled by the reichstag seize the initiative in directing the reich; or those more influenced by the direction of the Prussian *Landtag* seize the initiative in Prussia [we can answer the question of whether] the hegemony state in its reich policy aspect has its policy determined by reich organs [e.g., the reichstag and its affiliated bodies] or is "Great Prussian" ruled. The inner structure of the reich and its individual states [provinces] however ensure this latter direction, the Great Prussian character of reich direction, retains the upper hand (*überwiegt*)."

And so it can be seen that Weber begins this version of his 1918 hegemony reflections by using the term largely coterminously with state sovereignty, then moves on to consider which forces may or may not be hegemonic within the "hegemony state" Germany. Weber – as indicated above – is very likely not referring to an international hegemony seeking country, so far as Germany goes. He then goes on to claim that Prussia retains considerable autonomy inside Germany, autonomy from the reichstag and similar elected bodies and their organs. The example of the Great Prussian bureaucracy largely engulfing the Prussian provincial bureaucracy and thereafter largely ignoring elected officials has spread nation wide according to Weber, with rapidly-growing bureaucracies inside the member 'states' of Germany following the Prussian lead, and moreover displaying greater loyalty to the Great Prussian bureaucracy in Berlin than to their own elected officials. The Great Prussian bureaucracy, on this read, acts like an authentic hegemonic apparatus – directing the general parameters of public policy in areas in which its perceives itself as having an interest, and proceeding in significant part of the basis of ideology control, all the while effectively shielding many of its operations from public scrutiny. For this reason, Weber claims, Prussia is free to promulgate "an autocracy based on bureaucratic life ideals," (in Mommsen, 1974, p. 180), i.e., a hegemon's ideology or apparatus justification. Furthermore, in the "Germany's Future Form of State" article cited above, Weber made reference to Prussia's "hegemonic privileges" ([461]; Weber, 2006, p. 505; *KPS*, p. 203) in the *Bundesrat,* this contention also of some use in fine tuning the hegemony concept by contextualizing it with reference to Wilhelmian practices. On balance Weber is broadly familiar with hegemony ideas and practices as they came to be recognized in the 20th century, and hence connecting them to a particular group – Anglo-Saxons – should present no major challenge.

    ii *Anglo-Saxon Capital.* Anglo-Saxon capital as defined by Weber refers to the major English-speaking power – England – in the run-up to WWI; and the English-speaking power (USA) which seized the mantle of chief global protector of capitalism in 1917 and retained it into the 21st Century. Private property based production and distribution of goods and services was a constant in "the national community of the Anglo-Saxons" ([160]; Weber 2006, p. 213; KPS p. 65). Weber's concept was in several respects a useful step toward recognizing the actual hegemenon before, during and after WWI, namely the Anglo-Saxon capital globalizing hegemonic network, one financially grounded in the City of London/Wall Street axis, but never – strictly speaking – being confined to either venue by 1914.

Weber's failure to completely connect the dots between his hegemony idea and the Anglo-Saxon capital idea, said failure resulting from an inability to conceptualize the Anglo-Saxon capital hegemony network as a supra-state entity - i.e. a combination steering relations between states from above – becomes apparent when reviewing the sociologist's two chief characterizations of the original Anglo-Saxon power, England, during WWI. Such was the sociologist's initial source for the concept of Anglo-Saxon capital. There was no reason to think a supra-state entity and a national state would have the same policy priorities – and they didn't.

In Section 1, "The Triple Alliance and the Western Powers" of the December 1915 article "Bismarck's Foreign Policy and the Present" Weber describes England's role within the ostensible international relations structure. Seeking to counter Triple Entente and above all British propaganda about alleged German aggression and militarism (true modern propaganda – a combination of persuasion and attempt to lower the cognitive level of propaganda victims at the same time being a WWI British invention), Weber first criticizes Bismarck's Triple Alliance creation of 1882 as a typically German "purely defensive" ([113]; Weber, 2006, p. 165; *KPS* p. 30) arrangement, further commenting that "It was in no sense a policy of a 'greater Germany' " (ibid).

Weber's basic attitude toward British (Anglo-American) and Entente (the "bourgeois-imperialist Entente") allegations of German aggression and militarism from Bismarck to the Guns of August 1914 was: "Too bad we *weren't* aggressive." Operating from this perspective, he moves to the topic of Wilhelmian German acquisition of overseas territory and colonization, which – for British-Entente ideologues – constituted serious disruption of the international order. The sociologist noted "the absence of any capitalist interest" for German overseas acquisitions, since said acquisitions were small - smaller than England, Russia, France and even Belgium ([113]; Weber 2026 p. 166; KPS p. 131). Though Weber – in collaboration with his colleague Werner Sombart – demonstrated that German colonialism of the day had limited impact anywhere, he conceded the effectiveness of British-Entente propaganda on the issue in the article in question.

Even more effective – albeit more at the tactical nation-state level than at the supra-state level - was the specifically English propaganda related to the expansion of the German fleet after 1900 under Admiral Tirpitz. Concurrently with initial industrialization, England had developed an embryonic military-industrial complex encompassing urban workers dependent upon shipbuilding and related military production for a livelihood, especially in Liverpool. Weber might well have known there was a significant group of Englishmen susceptible to panic at the prospect of a German naval build-up, but he expressed astonishment at British propaganda success on the issue anyway. Weber noted that Germans had garnered the impression that "England, with regard to all overseas possibilities of Germany – including those in which significant British interests were in no way threatened – would nonetheless constantly assume a posture in opposition to us" ([115]; Weber 2006, p. 168; KPS p. 32). Reasoning from a tactical nation-state basis, not a supra-state network basis, Weber went on to observe that the English naval lead over the rest of the world was shrinking globally in the light of naval expansion everywhere; that the French fleet was far more likely to catch up with the British fleet in the near future than the German; and that the ambitious U.S.-Americans were likely to pass up England entirely in the near future so far as naval forces went – the latter of which of course took place. Some limitations of Weber's nation-state approach to global political analysis are apparent here. The first is the failure to differentiate useful scarecrow issues with the English masses – e.g., foreign naval build-ups - from actual policy grounds of state action. Another propaganda claim of the British government at the time – that (as reported by Weber) " 'every Englishmen will get richer' when Germany ceases to exist" ([114-115; Weber 2008 p. 167; *KPS* p. 31) cannot be looked upon as a policy ground (or even a sincerely-intended statement). In fact the British national government – the parliamentary body admired by Weber for its leadership selection processes – went to war for one reason only. It was ordered to do so from above by the the Anglo-Saxon capital hegemony network. The network in turn had only one lead motive – fear of hegemony loss. The grounds for the fear – concern about Central European labour; social jealousy of German scientific and cultural advance, with its possibilities for species advance of humanity; economic, industrial and population growth of Germany; and finally the geo-political threat to the network's international political enforcer (Russian Oriental despotism) posed by Germany and its allies in the Central Powers – were usually not the grounds advanced in public by the British government. Day-to-day tactics were as a rule left to the official government while the hegemonic network maintained the general course, above all preserving itself. The German sociologist's over-emphasis on national antagonisms led him – as Mommsen noted - to primarily blame pre-war German diplomacy (Mommsen 1974, p. 151) for Anglo-German strife when in fact British leaders were simply standing at attention awaiting network orders from above without paying any particular heed to German diplomats.

Weber's 1916 article discussing the English government sub-unit of the Anglo-Saxon capital hegemony network reveals limitations similar to the 1915 contribution discussed above. In "Germany under the European World Powers" he observes "It was not German competition that was the decisive ground for war but rather the perceived menace of our *fleet*. The average English philistine (*Spiessbürger*) feared the danger of a landing" ([165]; Weber 2006 p. 218; *KPS* p. 70). Of course average philistines don't make state policy; nationalistic motives don't necessarily steer things either. Although admitting the war lines between England and Germany had been clearly drawn, Weber waxed fairly optimistically in 1916 about possibilities of Anglo-German naval rapprochement, this owing to continual lack of German aggressive propensities. The sociologist wrote that "Since Germany only needs a defensive fleet, a change in this state of affairs is not foreclosed" ([166]; Weber 2006 p. 218; *KPS* p. 70). What counted for the Anglo-Saxon capital hegemony network was ensuring no further German-led (or any other) Continental European threat to its control could arise. Though the naval disarmament of Germany after the war (scuttling of ships at Scapa Flow) was welcome to the network, restoring English naval dominance meant nothing special to it. The upstart U.S. Navy could serve just as well (or better).

And so it can be seen that Weber's aforementioned failure to connect the dots between his hegemony theory and his depiction of Anglo-Saxon capital generated mistakes more than once. In evaluations of the respective careers of David Lloyd George and Raymond Poincaré in 1919 ([584-585]; Weber 2006 p. 562; see Excursus to follow) Weber projects a belief that the two political leaders were acting independently of any supervening network, both in the run-up to the world war and at Versailles in 1919. In reality the two were largely mannequins for the U.S. President Woodrow Wilson, designated director of the Anglo-Russian secret diplomacy state, at the Versailles Conference and there is little reason to believe they were more independent of the network prior to August 1914.

But once the Weberian hegemony concept and his Anglo-Saxon capital formation idea are integrated with the encirclement policy hypothesis referenced by the sociologist in 1919 ([496]; Weber 2006 p. 530; *KPS* p. 232) as well as with recognition of the hegemony loss anxiety phenomenon so commonly present in history in the case of declining powers, analytic possibilities are many. Such is in fact a promising approach to understanding the contemporary Ukraine-Germany-Russia alignment and the related potential world-historical decline and fall of Anglo-Saxon capital hegemonic pretension, this in conjunction with the decline and fall of its final organizational sword and buckler, the American Empire.

MAX WEBER SECTION SUMMARY. A readily reconstructed model of Germany in the era of the Great War, 1914-1919 based on Weber's political writings indicates that the Anglo-Saxon capital hegemony network – not a state but a supra-state entity organized in defense of private property in production globally by the English-speaking peoples – pursued an encirclement tactic (See Map 2) in attacking Germany and its allies in 1914 (above all via its international relations attack dog Czarist Russia), the entire constellation of actions being based on a realistic appraisal that an ascendant German-led Continental Bloc constituted a threat to its hegemony. Again drawing on Weber, a model encompassing all the important factors – Anglo-Saxon hegemonic capital; encirclement tactic; pre-selected victim; German as well as Russian involvement in the struggle; and hegemony loss anxiety propelling the action – can be developed. Amazingly enough, every one of these factors in present in the 2022-2023 Ukraine situation. Thus Anglo-Saxon hegemonic capital, working through its 20th century sword and buckler, the U.S., has attacked Russia and Russian Ukraine utilizing the encirclement tactic and exploiting its Germany-based attack dog (NATO) in advancing its aggression project based on the quite accurate assessment that the targeted victim – Russia (now in firm alliance with China and the BRICS tendency) – represents a threat to the network's hegemony worldwide. That a model derived from Weber's work – all of it a century old at the minimum – displays such explanatory reach in the contemporary context suggested the appropriateness of an at least preliminary reconstruction of Weber's concept of state and politics. The reconstruction first addressed the aspect of Russia-Prussia analogies in Weber's political writings. The sociologist's engagement with Russian affairs pursuant to his 1905-1906 monographs on the 1905 Russian Revolution left a permanent mark on his overall project of characterizing the Wilhelmian-Prussian state, 1871-1919 and as a practical matter he was operating with a bi-polar conception of Russian despotism bad/British constitutionalism good while conducting analysis, this despite unquestionable sympathy for Russian emancipation movements, movements continually set back by Anglo-Saxon (and French) capital's ceaseless support for the worst aspects of Russian autocracy. The second point was Weber's historicist insistence that the peculiar concantenation of liberal-individualist values and industrial capitalist development in the latter European 19th century couldn't possibly be repeated in 20th century Russia (or anywhere). By the 20th century the results of capitalist industrialization could be inserted into numerous national contexts without any necessarily emancipatory consequences, Weber insisted, indicating deterministic confidence economic history was moving global

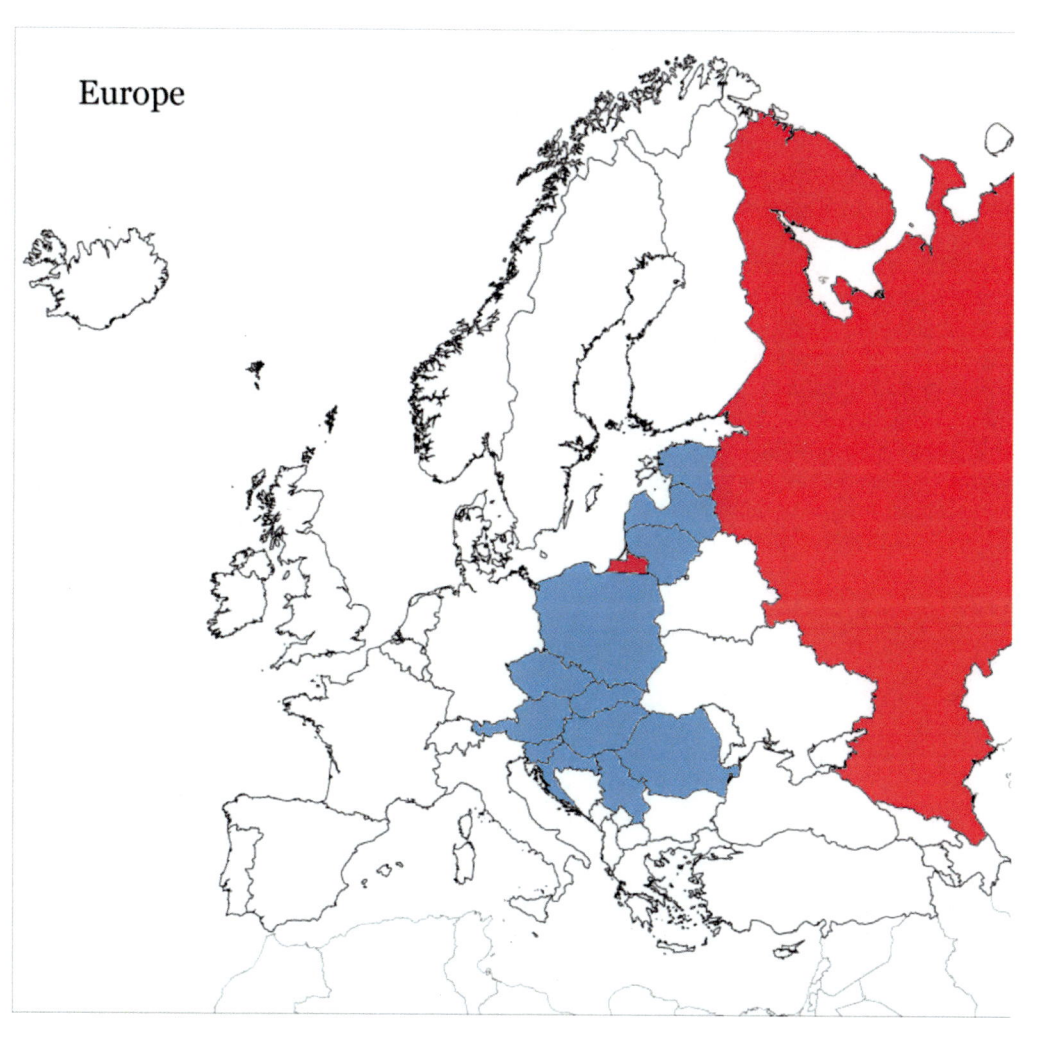

Map 2 The Bucharest Nine Encirclement of the Russian Federation in 2023

development in a liberal-individualist direction was not just naive – it was dangerous. Weber's third concern was to point the finger of blame for starting WWI away from Germany and toward Czarist Russia, this utilizing the appropriate method of placing the conflict's outbreak in long-range perspective of years and decades prior to the war, rather than just focusing on short-range diplomatic manuevers in the Summer of 1914 as Triple Entente/Allied efforts to vilify Germany usually did. The sociologist's long list of factors conditioning Czarist aggression included 'people's imperialism' driven by land hunger of culturally deprived peasants; wishes of foreign credit holders of the Russian 'creditor's state'; and the traditional capacity for aggression of the Sino-Mongol Russian bureaucracy. The final factor in delineating Weber's political analysis was in part reconstructive. It sought to synthesize his notions of Anglo-Saxon capital with hegemony (the latter derived from examination of Great Prussian bureaucracy) to bring into relief that neither England nor the U.S. (contrary to Weber's indications) ever commanded the Triple Entente war effort; it was steered from above by the non-state network Anglo-Saxon hegemonic capital, which was largely indifferent as to which state it would delegate authority to act on a particular issue, if it cared to delegate. From the reconstructed Weberian perspective the Leninist imperialism interpretation of WWI – according to which the conflict was one between the ruling classes of states (and moreover culturally similar states) - was invalid from two directions at once. The main (and victorious) party, the Anglo-Saxon hegemonic capital network, was no state of any kind. Secondly the exotic, 'Asiatic' character of Russian despotism meant the Czarist regime couldn't possibly be grouped culturally with Western regimes, no matter what its financial dependency on some of them. Indeed it might well have been a specific intent of foreign financiers to preserve aspects of Russian 'otherness.'

EXCURSUS

Weber's Thesis the February 1917 Revolution in Russia
was simply "The elimination of an incapable monarch" and no revolution.
Laying the groundwork for Lenin's Wall Street
"Re-Russification" (de-Occidentalization) plan for October 1917

Weber's contention in the article "The Prussian Electoral Law" of April 21, 1917 (Weber 2006, pp. 244-251) that - contrary to U.S.-American press declarations that a 'revolution' had taken place and a 'republic' had been installed in Russia in the wake of the abdication of the Czar - nothing had happened in the Russia of February of 1917 except "the *purely technical . . . elimination* of an incapable monarch" (Weber, 2006, p. 244), this resulting in a regime as dependent upon foreign financiers and as hell-bent on continuing the war effort as the Czarist version had been, was subjected to criticism in the latter 20th century by Richard Pipes and Wolfgang J. Mommsen. In the "Parliament and Government in Newly Ordered Germany" contribution of the Summer of 1918 ([337]; Weber 2006, p. 374) Weber reiterated his critique of the Kerensky Regime of 1917 as the plaything of foreign (read: Anglo-Saxon) capital, such evidenced above all by the bitter determination of Kerensky to continue the Russian war effort. In the April 1917 article Weber dwelt on the impeccable anti-democratic credentials of those who carried out the recent ouster of the Czar, writing that (Weber, 2006, pp. 244-245) "The leaders of the 'revolution' were monarchists, great landowners and behind the scenes indeed grand service princes. . . . These thoroughly anti-democratic circles of Russian imperialists overcame the old regime while acting upon purely *objective* grounds. . . They needed . . . the *credit* of both domestic as well as international banks to organize power. . . This 'democracy' is therefore pure Humbug and we have *absolutely nothing* to "learn" from this swindle. . . . The new regime is in the last analysis - for us - the old regime with a new name."

Weber's distinctive view of the post-February Kerensky regime in Russia then, was that it was a stepping stone to Bolshevik totalitarianism necessitated by the need to remove a Czarist monarchy which was losing its capacity to play attack dog against threats to the Wall Street/City of London axis (the Anglo-Saxon capital hegemony network), this whether the threats originated in Germany or anywhere else. The dilemma of Czarist circles in St. Petersburg in January of 1917 on the eve of their ouster by Wall Street was indeed acute. Still well funded from the West and constantly urged to continue war on the Central Powers by Entente forces, the huge funds Anglo-Saxon capital was providing the Bolsheviks - this with an eye to governmental takeover by the Lenin entourage in October - could hardly remain hidden from the Czar's circle. Indeed when the February Revolution broke out Lenin's chief lieutenant Leon Trotsky was in New York lining up additional funding from the Rockefellers and other Wall Street sources. The Wall Street press ballyhoo about democracy arising in Russia after February (as mocked by Weber) was designed both to ease the U.S. entry into the war (providing a progressive patina for Russian bureaucratic despotism) and obscure the continuity in Russian affairs pre- and post-February. The Wall Street installation of Lenin as Russian head of state was carried out on schedule in October, and the dispersal at gun point of the Constituent Assembly in January of 1918 by Bolshevik forces was – as Weber observed - the end of any electoral democracy in Russia (no matter how formal).[24]

---

[24] Regarding the extinction of electoral democracy in Russia by the Bolsheviks, Weber observed in the "Domestic State of Affairs and Foreign Policy" article of February 3, 1918 ([293]; Weber 2006 p. 168; *KPS* p. 168) that "The sole, i.e. at least formally via democratic elections legitimated authority in Russia - the Constituent Assembly - was broken up by force of violence."

Weber's position on the February Revolution attracted the negative attention of several critics, including veteran Harvard University historian Richard Pipes (1923-2018) and Wolfgang J. Mommsen (1930-2004). The discussion, as reconstructed by Mommsen,[25] upheld Pipes' contention that Weber had something of a phobia regarding popular revolution - or any mass mobilizations - since the German sociologist regarded such movements as street-based, disorderly, proto-Russian/Bonapartist (always a serious rebuke for Weber) and prone to manipulation by hidden elite forces. Mommsen criticized Weber's interpretation of the February Russian revolution as being so tendentious that it couldn't be characterized as a scientific treatment.[26] In fairness to Weber, it must be observed that neither of the critics really engaged with the sociologist's two main items of evidence, namely foreign capital control and continuity of the Russian national war effort. No matter how much Lenin's Bolsheviks spoke of revolutionary defeatism and the need for peace, the war effort continued until well after U.S. entry into the conflict in Summer of 1917 decided the outcome. The consolidation of Bolshevik control after 1917 was followed by a massive foreign aid program from the U.S. Government, this in addition to the funding provided privately by the New York banks. When Soviet dictator Josef Stalin answered a summons to journey to the City of London in 1923 to receive his training in running the eastern end of the Anglo-Russian secret diplomacy state – following in the footsteps of Lenin in 1902 (Reference 2) and Peter the Great in 1697 – he encountered California businessman Herbert C. Hoover, who briefed the Georgian on the selfsame Hoover's ambitious bread-for-despotism program carried out in the Bolshevik Russia of the 1920s, one which saved the Bolshevik regime from ruin on numerous occasions. Hoover was rewarded with the U.S. White House in 1928 for his efforts. Weber would have been the last to be surprised at the continuity of Anglo-Saxon capital influence in Russia in the decades after he penned the "Prussian Electoral Law" piece of April 1917.

Excursus Summary

Weber's expectations that the Bolshevik regime would be short-lived were clearly disappointed, but he did recognize that changes had taken place in Russia after October 1917, even if none of

---

25 Mommsen, 1974, pp. 274-276, et seq.
26 Ibid. Mommsen noted that Weber's prediction of limited longevity of the Bolshevik Regime did not hold true, as did Hans-Peter Müller (Müller, 2020, p. 296).

them pointed in a democratic direction. He noted that "Bolshevik soldier-imperialism – so long as it is extant – endangers the security and self-determination of all countries bordering Russia, and it is highly unlikely that a government dependent upon such militaristic mass instincts *could* make a proper peace at all, even if it wanted to" ([293]; Weber 2006 p. 338; *KPS* p. 168). He stated further that "Whether an imperialist expansion drive is conducted with Czarist, Cadet or Bolshevist slogans is, so far as practical effect goes, a matter of complete indifference" (ibid).

In light of Weber's research, the fate of the February Revolution of 1917 ended by the October Revolution and followed by the dispersal of the January 1918 Constituent Assembly can be depicted. When Lenin's storm troopers broke up the Constituent Assembly at gun point, it was the culmination of a systematic Wall Street plan. The Czar had been removed in February since the Anglo-Russian capital hegemony network wanted a much more dynamic attack dog for its international projects than the archaic Czarist regime, a regime too porous to Western and democratic influences to suit the network's tastes, and moreover something of a public relations liability so far as dragging the USA into the war was concerned. The chaos of the February-October period was ideally suited to setting up machinery for long-run Bolshevik rule. After the Constituent Assembly was dispersed, the road was clear for Soviet Russia to service the Anglo-Saxon network for some 75 years so long as Western public and private subsidies to keep it going kept flowing – which they did. Services rendered for the network by the Bolsheviks were numerous. They aided in undermining Germany's Weimar Republic (1919-1933); divided the world labour movement into social-democratic and communist claimants; provided a cover for huge warfare state expenditures in the Cold War West; and also provided a convenient excuse for the network's agents to supress liberation movements everywhere by calling them communist. Max Weber's contemporaneous analysis of Russian developments in the 1917-1918 period has been little improved upon by the analyses which followed it.

III. The Russian Federation
in Ukraine, 2022-2023

As noted in The Peace of Utrecht. Origins of Neo-Chinggisid International Relations Structures 1713-1998[27], the Anglo-Russian Secret Diplomacy state consolidated by Peter the Great and English King George I of Hanover circa 1714 came to a end at the ascendancy of Vladimir Putin (b. 1952) to the position of Russian chief of state in 1998. The secret diplomacy state as identified by Marx in the 1850s constituted a diplomatic structure mediating (when necessary) between the Anglo-Saxon capital hegemony network and nation states such as England. When the network became truly multi-centered geographically with the integration of Wall Street into it at the outset of the 20th century, the secret diplomacy state continued to function. By the end of the 1990s however Vladimir Putin and his entourage came to the well-informed conclusion that the network was seeking to organize a new world order without Russia as a major power in it. The decision to break the yoke of servitude to Anglo-Saxon capital going back to Czar Peter I was a momentous one for the Russians, but the view that there was no alternative if Russia were to continue to play a world role was quite justified

Initial Western (i.e., U.S.) response to what has turned out to be the most revolutionary change in Russia history in more than three centuries appeared subdued. Anglo-Saxon capital forces initially developed a staged plan to increase economic penetration of Western capital into the Russian Federation while gradually building up NATO encirclement of Russia, this to achieve the mid-run goal of reducing the Federation to satellite status (or even breaking it up into small national units). Sufficient sophistication to understand the plan at the Russian end as well as the will of the Putin group to resist it, were quite underestimated by Western intelligence. But the decision from the West to concentrate the attack on Russia in Ukraine was made, and a situation remarkably similar to that of Germany in 1914 was created (see chart to follow).

Examination of the chart reveals most of the variables in play in Europe at the Guns of August 1914 and in Ukraine 2022-2023 are the same. The chief actuator-aggressor in both case is the Anglo-Saxon capital hegemony network. The network's primary motive in both cases is quite understandable global hegemony loss anxiety. The network's organizational sword and buckler both times is the USA. Lead tactic in both contexts is encirclement of the victim-state. In both cases a special state attack dog - which is not exactly the same as the organizational sword and

---

[27] Drischler, 2022, pp. 43-44.

	August 1914 in Europe	vs.	2022-2023 in Ukraine
Actuator of the conflict	Anglo-Saxon Capital Hegemony Network		Anglo-Saxon Capital Hegemony Network
Sword and Buckler of the Actuator	USA		USA
Chief Tactic of the Actuator	Encirclement		Encirclement
Chief Motive of the Actuator	Hegemony Loss Anxiety		Hegemony Loss Anxiety
Chief Strategy of the Actuator	Deployment of State Attack Dog (Czarist Russia)		Deployment of state Attack Dog (Germany-based NATO)
Projected chief victim	Germany		Russian Federation

buckler - is being deployed strategically. Although the intended main encirclement victims – in 1914 Germany and in 2022-2023 the Russian Federation – as well as the respective attack dogs deployed (Czarist Russia in 1914 and German-led NATO forces in 2020-2023) differ, the 2022 contentions of Stefan Bollinger in The Russians are Coming! that the current military action in the Ukraine is far from unprecedented and that the 1914 Europe analogy is potentially quite useful as a clarification source in the situation (the latter view widespread in today's Continental Europe) are credible. In the chapter "Opportunities and Pacts with the Devil" in The Russians are Coming! Bollinger chose to attempt to tie his entire interpretation together with reference to the Treaty of Rapallo of April 16, 1922 between the Soviet Union and Weimar Germany.

a. Stephan Bollinger's Rapallo Treaty Analogy

A reconstruction of Bollinger's Rapallo treaty analogy would be as follows.[28] So far the as the nation-state level of European politics in 1922 went, the Soviet Union and Weimar Germany were widely perceived as twin pariahs and the by all appearances sincere attempt of the two national powers to bring about a rapprochement featuring increased trade ties and cultural exchange at Rapallo were perceived as suggesting quasi-independence from the Versailles Treaty victors in Europe as typified by the two Entente 'statesmen' discussed above, namely David Lloyd George of Britain and Raymond Poincaré of France. As Wall Street – to use another canine figure of speech – running dogs, George and Poincaré feared any modification of the Versailles reparations system expressly designed to hamstring both German economic growth and sovereignty consolidation. In order to score points in New York, Poincaré concocted a crackpot scheme for novel reparations payments to be made to the Soviet Union by Germany, after which the Bolsheviks were to re-route the special funds back to French capital to repay decades of loans from France to Czarist Russian despotism (Reference 51). The last thing possible the Bolsheviks

---

[28] A problem with reconstructing his 2022 discussion is that Bollinger – like many under the spell of World War II propaganda produced by the U.S. non-stop from 1945 to today - can barely make a single observation about the 1922 situation in Europe without racing forward to World War II and German fascism for a comparison. This is part of the popular U.S. re-interpretation of German history after 1945 according to which all of German history prior to 1933 is a lead-up to Hitler, and everything afterwards is a footnote to Hitler. This pathological U.S. popular Hitler obsession consistently evades the Anglo-Austrian dictator's well-documented status as a salaried U.S. agent, documented above all by Anthony Sutton in his Wall Street and the Rise of Hitler (2010 ed.).

wanted at the time was to assume old Czarist debt – the Soviets were focused on obtaining novel subsidies from the Entente-Allied countries (or anywhere else). The psychological lift provided by the manuevering room the Rapallo powers had garnered for themselves became known as 'the spirit of Rapallo'- with positive connotations in Central Europe and negative ones in Paris, New York and London. Bollinger summarizes by observing that "Indeed the treaty of April 16, 1922 was an alternative . . . above all to [the Treaty] . . . of Versailles" (127). A major reason Rapallo constituted an alternative to the Versailles Treaty was that the Versailles Treaty wasn't a treaty so far as Germany went – it was a *diktat.* German representatives weren't even allowed into the negotiating room in 1919.

But better treatment for Germany wasn't the 'magic' of Rapallo for Bollinger. The magic was major benefits for Bolshevik Russia. The German political scientist observed that the Soviet Union had seized an opportunity at Rapallo that had "led the way to a more secure alliance in the future. Moscow's success in the matter was unquestionably more spectacular than that of Germany . . . . At the end of the day the Soviet state was not just formally but practically recognized as an equal party in international law" (126). The nub of Bollinger's critique of what he termed "German hysteria" (*deutsche Hysterie*) engendered at the initiation of the Russian Special Military Operation in Ukraine in February of 2022 is that it signaled a dissipation of the advantages of a Rapallo style agreement, a regression to treating the leading Eastern Slav nation as a pariah nation, said course of conduct being one replete with disadvantages for Germany and Europe. The WWI mobilization cry "The Russians are Coming" is seen as *inappropos* in the Germany (or Central Europe) of today since among other things the WWII losses in Russia were of unparalleled dimensions and hence Russian perceptions of secure borders must be respected. Emotional revulsion at a new round of war, it is said, should not be allowed to lead to regressions in international relations which would ultimately provoke further military confrontations. However German over-reaction to 2022 hostilities cannot really compare to possible permanent nation-state hegemony loss for the USA and the forces behind it as a factor related to continuation of the conflict.

b. Is Anglo-Saxon hegemony doomed?

i *Multi-Polarity Coagulation.* In his 2022 discussion of the prospects for U.S./Anglo-Saxon hegemony decline, Bollinger makes reference to a 2022 work by publicist Peter Wahl[29] as follows.

> The publicist Peter Wahl has made reference to the readily-apparent end of the post 1989-1991 unipolar, U.S.-led world order as a disruption which unquestionably leads to dangerous turbulences and conflicts. In the place of the previous world order 'a multipolar system is emerging. In its center one finds the rivalry between the U.S. and China. Simultaneously there is a comeback of Russia as a great power. India is also seeking to ascend to the status of a super power. The conflict between unipolar and multipolar orders has assumed increasing importance for almost a decade at the center of international systems.'

The difference between the world state of affairs in 2022 as commented upon by Wahl and Bollinger and the Spring of 2023 is that multipolarity, i.e., the end of U.S. nation-state hegemony, is at hand – not a trend – and this will mean that the posterior monolithic hegemony of the Anglo-Saxon capital hegemony network in place in Europe since the Peace of Utrecht treaties of the 1713-1721 era and in place globally since Lord Palmerston's 2nd Opium War in 1859 will be coming to an end with the dissolution of the role of the network's final organizational sword and buckler – the U.S. Empire. There is no alternative English-speaking nation with an iota of the strategic wherewithal to project global hegemony against the now consolidated Sino-Russian bloc. The critically important aspect of the situation is that the ascendant multipolarity camp has always had to live with subordination to English-speakers' hegemony and is enjoying the bracing

---

29 Peter Wahl, *"Der Ukraine-Krieg und seine geopolitischen Hintergründe. Hintergrundpapier Nr. 1, vom 18. März 2022 (Redaktionsschluss)" Attac AG Globalisierung & Krieg. Frankfurt/M*, p. 2 (28; 220).

experience of ascendancy for the first time.. The declining power however has had no experience with sliding downwards dramatically and may simply dissolve, being too deeply accustomed to being on top to adjust to the changed situation. When the ancient Assyrian Empire deflated it became unknown in just a few years, and was forgotten until the 19th century. Though constantly preaching the virtues of a polycentric world, the Anglo-Saxon capital hegemony network did everything imaginable to prevent such a world from coming about – and this for more than a century. Who is playing the lead role in bringing all this to an end? One name will do – Mother Russia.

As indicated above, the actual structure of the Anglo-Saxon capital hegemony network had three layers. First was the actual network, conducting affairs in secret and initially operating in the City of London only. Beneath that was yet another secret apparatus – the Anglo-Russian secret diplomacy state exposed by Marx in his 1850s anti-Palmerston polemics.[30] The aristocrat Palmerston was ideally suited to mediating between the two structures. The grandees at the top were disinclined to deal on an equal footing with ordinary elected officials and preferred to work through the secret diplomacy state. Beneath this was the initial leading nation-state, England. When after 1900 the grandees at the top in London indicated the U.S. (Wall Street) was acceptable as a supplemental organizational sword and buckler to the U.K., the imprimatur for U.S. inclusion was proffered, this under the strict condition that the Anglo-Russian secret diplomacy structure continue undisturbed. U.S. agreement was prompt. American President James Buchanan (the last slavery president)(in office 1853-1861) was a long-identified Russian espionage agent, having spent most of the 1832-1833 years kneeling at the feet of the Russian Czar in St. Petersburg receiving one-on-one political tutoring. As mentioned above, Marx indicated in his "Value, Price and Profit" pamphlet that the Russians initiated the U.S. civil war, very likely in concert with Buchanon. The Anglo-Saxon network expansion to include a North American center went smoothly, and when German military prowess in WWI damaged England's strategic capacity, Wall Street bought into the entire package – Anglo-Saxon capital hegemony network; Anglo-Russian secret diplomacy state; and alliance with England – and the U.S. became the leading nation-state promulgating world domination for the English-speaking peoples.

---

30 Drischler, "Marx and Russia.etc", in Drischler 2019

It was not until the end of the 1990s however that U.S. strategists began to grasp the fact that City of London insistence on a Russia-integrated secret state structure circa 1900 was no British pecadillo. With China as a credible multipolarity ally, the Putin regime saw the chance to opt out of economic and technological dependency on the Anglo-Saxon-led West, and opt out it did, ending an arrangement that stretched back to Czar Peter I. Based on astute perceptions that the novel Sino-Russian block had the potential to bring in what the Anglo-Saxon bloc had always advocated but never practiced – multipolarity – the U.S. stepped up military pressure on the Russian Federation through NATO, particularly by seeking to transform Ukraine into an armed camp, all the while pursuing with great confidence various monetary and fiscal ploys to cut the Russian Federation down to size or even eliminate it. By the Spring of 2023 however the Russia-favorable de facto cease fire in Ukraine meant the NATO coalition and its string pullers had failed militarily. Failure begets failure, and it has turned out that global de-dollarization is now playing an even bigger role in ending the Anglo-Saxon hegemony unit than anything that has occurred on the battlefield.

ii BRICS De-dollarization accelerates Anglo-Saxon Decline. The April 21, 2023 English RT blog "BRICS de-dollarization push gaining momentum – Jakarta. The new economic bloc of nations has been working on establishing a new reserve currency" illustrates the accelerating dissolution of the 70s petro dollar/1945 Breton Woods monetary and economic foundation of U.S. nation-state hegemony globally. As just observed, this dissolution will contribute to the end of the global Anglo-Saxon hegemony network as well because the U.S. and its current allies by all appearances cannot stand up to the relentlessly expanding BRICS [Brazil-Russia-China-South Africa] alignment and there is no state actor to take the place of the U.S.

With the world's fourth highest population (280 million people), the official announcement that Indonesia is ditching the U.S. dollar as a currency exchange medium made by Bank of Indonesia President Perry Warjiyo on April 21 is a stunning setback to the dollar. In a blunt statement at a press conference, Warjiyo observed that "Indonesia has initiated diversification of the use of currency in the form of LCT [local currency trading]. The direction is the same as BRICS. In fact, Indonesia is more concrete." *Eminence grise* for the BRICS currency movement is Russian president Putin, who – according to the RT blog – has suggested that after ditching the dollar for local currency exchanges BRICS countries might consider adopting the Chinese Yuan as a new universal currency. With a population approaching 2.5 billion, the BRICS countries' desertion of the dollar will likely constitute the greatest exchange currency modification in history. The course of recent centuries confirms that national, regional and especially global hegemony cannot function without currency control, and U.S./Anglo-Saxon global currency control is currently spinning out of control.

FINAL REVIEW & CONCLUSIONS

Military conflict in Ukraine 2022-2023 has had undeniable impact. Yet behind the conduct of hostilities lies a larger issue – the global hegemony revolution taking place as the USA loses its place as the hegemonic super-power nation state, and with its decline the much older Anglo-Saxon capital hegemony network - resting on a globalized Anglo-Russian secret diplomacy state which mediated between the originary Anglo-Saxon network and whichever national power (or powers) was organizationally prominent – faces extinction. The ascendant powers stepping rapidly into the breach precipitated by U.S. decline include the Sino-Russian bloc and its affiliated BRICS trading partners, partners which are de-dollarizing their trade practices with speed and thoroughness and already represent billions of people.

Although ultimately of subordinate significance to the hegemony revolution, the Ukraine conflict – taking place at the nexus of Ukraine-Germany-Russia – is the ideal portal from which to acquire perspective on developments.

The sequence of military events in Ukraine in 2022 – bold initiatives at the outset, followed by territorially insignificant changes accompanied by massive losses in an attrition struggle – seemed to German and other observers to bear an uncomfortable resemblance to the trench warfare of 1914-1916 in France. The analogy was in fact very suggestive and Berlin political scientist Stefan Bollinger sought to draw it out in his 2022 German work *The Russians are Coming!* The very title of the volume brought into relief Bollinger's intent. The slogan 'The Russians are Coming!' was a mobilization phrase from 1914 expressing Germans' desire to make the world safe from Russian despotism and its Anglo-French financial sponsors. Bollinger's purpose was to create as much understanding for the Russian Federation as was feasible in the situation and defuse anti-Russian militancy in the German public. This was the general posture of Bollinger's political party - the Party of the Left - the main successor organization of the former East German Communist Party (*SED*), though some members of the Party initially expressed sympathy for attempts to vilify the Russian Federation organized by the Western mass media and supported by the governing Ampel coalition of Social democrats, Liberals and Greens. Strengths of the 2022

Bollinger work included stress on the WW I analogy; reminding the public the Ukraine conflict was in many respects a routine war in Europe; and insisting the outbreak of the conflict was similar to previous ones in that it was brought about by long-run factors manipulated by parties and persons in some cases far removed from the fighting front. On balance Bollinger had produced several diamonds of wisdom.

But as G.W.F. Hegel (1770-1831) was wont to observe, with the diamonds comes the dung. Surprisingly for a German social scientist, Bollinger in the 2022 work systematically evaded the scholarship of the leading social scientist of the 20th century, one who – owing to having conducted highly specialized work on the Wilhelmian state and early 20th-century Russia as well – is considered a major source world-wide for clarifying the roles of Germany and Russia in the Great War and in fact produced a stream of publications dealing with policy aspects of the German and Central powers war effort as it was unfolding. Bollinger provided no explanation for his Max Weber evasion, but its effects on his analysis were palpable. Consistent with its author's communist background, The Russians are Coming! operates with what could be termed a 'selective Leninist' paradigm. Lenin's WWI contention that all the major combatant powers were 'imperialist' entailed the assertion that all the powers had similar motives of expanding market shares, extending colonialism and improving access to raw materials, and what's more were steering a conflict based above all on collision of nation-state ruling classes. In light of his predisposition to blame Germany and Germans for igniting the 1914 conflict, Bollinger had marched straight into contradiction land by embracing a neo-Leninist conceptual framework, since a Germany which hardly differed in war motives from the other powers could scarcely have had unique culpability for staging the conflict. Lenin's version of imperialism analysis did not feature such a contradiction, but did feature several other gaping holes. The leading – and victorious – power in the WWI conflict was no state and hence did not feature a national ruling class. Rather it was the Anglo-Saxon capital hegemonic network, which worked through the U.S. national government and the British government (and the French government) as it pleased. In any major conflict, the anatomy of the victor is more important than the anatomy of the vanquished, and the network certainly wasn't a nation-state. Lead motive of the victor wasn't primarily economic either – it was hegemony loss anxiety, which (even if it had economic repercussions) couldn't be narrowly economic. The network's hegemony was threatened by the pre-WWI Central European labour movement; German technological and cultural leadership which raised questions of 'species boost' to a higher form of humanity (See Afterword); German industrial and population growth after unification in 1871; and the threat a unified Germany represented to the networks' much-favored gendarme cum attack dog, Czarist Russia. Missing the main party to the world war entirely was quite a hole in the analysis of Lenin and Bollinger, but there was another one of parallel importance – failing to realize Czarist Russia with its Russo-Asiatic mode of production (as clarified by Marx and K.A. Wittfogel) was non-European and kept that way by the Anglo-Russian capital hegemony group, and hence couldn't be expected to behave in the manner of a Western power - and did not do so.

Not only can most of the limitations of the Lenin-Bollinger imperialism interpretation be cleared up by just one author – Weber. Most can be corrected by reference to just one volume – the widely-used 1988 5th German edition of Weber' political writings edited by Johannes Winckelmann. The main features of Weber's political theory included first of all extensive use of Russia analogies regarding most political matters. The sociologist's 1905-1906 immersion in Russia studies proved invaluable in charting the course of events in the Great War, since he was operating with very much better information on Russian affairs than most European publicists. A fundamental insight of Weber's "On the State of Bourgeois Democracy in Russia" monograph from the 1905-1906 period is that the historical sequence from liberal individualist values to (potentially) emancipatory industrialization experienced in the West was unrepeatable afterward, and hence the tendency of some to leap to the conclusion Russia was being democratized by the appearance of some industry (or, later, by the ouster of Czar) was quite naive. Weber's contention of geniune heterogeneity of Czarist Russia in comparison to Western Europe centered about his concept (borrowed from Austro-Marxism) of a 'people's imperialism' of land-hungry Russian peasants, as well as numerous other factors fueling Russian aggression. Weber's perspective on Czarist Russia during the Great War differs very widely from that of Lenin and Bollinger in that the German sociologist placed stress on the political role of the bureaucracy, rejecting the implausible assertion of Leninists that the real confrontation in the Russia of the WW I era was between bourgeoisie and proletariat. For Weber, the Russian bureaucracy completely eclipsed the bourgeoisie before WWI, and the Russia peasantry dwarfed the urban working class, the latter minority group consisting mostly of recently transplanted rural hayseeds.

The next step in forging an authoritative Weberian interpretation of today's Ukraine-Germany-Russia situation - this on the path to understanding today's global hegemony revolution - required some reconstruction. Although Weber makes frequent reference to Anglo-Saxon capital in the political writings edited by Winckelmann in 1988, and discussed hegemony problems related to the Great Prussian bureaucracy in the 1916-1918 interregnum as well, he failed to decisively link the two. If the sociologist had developed an integrated Anglo-Saxon capital hegemony network concept in the manner later suggested by Gramsci, outlining the actual parallels between the trenches in Flanders' fields in 1916 and in Ukraine today would have been facilitated, which would in turn have facilitated outlining of today's hegemony revolution. As indicated above, in Ukraine 2022-2023 the Anglo-Saxon capital network and its U.S. organizational sword and buckler have made a last stand. The 1998 collapse of the Anglo-Russian secret diplomacy state prop holding up the network as a whole is leading to the network's disintegration now. The Russian former prop cum gendarme for the network sees greener pastures in alliance with the PRC, and nations around the world can see that China is the wave of future. None of these developments need be surprising for those acquainted with the concepts of Sino-Russian affinities, Anglo-Saxon capital and hegemony as developed by Max Weber.

Appendix

Oriental Despotism and August 1914

Reprinted from *The Appeal to Reason.*
A Social Democratic Quarterly,
No. 25, Spring 1980,
James T. Burnett, Ed.,
Walnut Creek, California

The subtitle originally submitted with the article - "Rosa Luxemburg, Lenin and the Outbreak of the First World War" - was deleted by the editor.

" . . . the semi-Asiatic politico-cultural character of Czarism . . . will stamp out the culture of the whole of Europe . . . . "

SPD Deputy Eduard David in the German Reichstag, August, 1914, Quoted in Abraham Berlau, *German Social Democracy 1912-1921*

"Ever since 1848 . . . Marx. . . had been preaching war with Russia, for he believed such a war would be a most powerful engine of the revolution."

Boris Nicolaievsky and Otto Menschen-Helfen in *Karl Marx: Man and Fighter*

"General conditions in Europe are of such a kind that they are heading more and more toward a general European war. We must go through it before there can be any thought of the European working classes having decisive influence."

Marx (letter to Sorge of 4 April 1874)

: . . . the Czar could only be overturned in a war with another great power. The foundations on which Russian absolutism rested were still too strong to be shaken by anything less than a European war . . . Anyone who fought Russia was objectively fighting in the service of the revolution."

Boris Nicolaievsky and Otto Maenschen-Helfen in *Karl Marx. Man and Fighter*

"At the end of the 19th century all . . . empires of Asia had a similar organizational structure called Asiatic despotism, which was quite unlike that of Western civilization."

Carroll Quigley in *Tragedy and Hope*

August 4, 1914: The German Working Class
Declares War upon Oriental Despotism in its
Most Insidious (Russian) Form

Karl A. Wittfogel has essentially demolished the Leninist-Stalinist these of Western-style "feudalism" in Russian history, showing the thesis to be a variance with both orthodox Marxism and empirical reality.[31] Juergen Habermas, a writer who has never been accused of doctrinaire anti-communism, felt compelled to state that by Marxist or any other rational standard, Lenin was no philosopher.[32] It is high time anti-totalitarian leftists applied similar critical scrutiny to the Leninist theory that the majority socialist movement in Central Europe "betrayed" its ideals by making war upon Russian Oriental despotism and its supporters amongst Western capital in 1914. Marx's analysis of "semi-Asiatic Russian barbarism" and the network of European reaction it undergirded[33] points unmistakably to the conclusion that he would have given unreserved support to the German national war effort in WWI, i.e., adopted the exact position of the majority socialists of the SPD on August 4, 1914. If Marx could give qualified support to Prussia against France in the Franco-Prussian War[34] on the grounds that the German national unity resulting from

---

31 See W.F. Drischler, "Karl A. Wittfogel's Theory of Oriental Despotism," in *The New International Review,* Vol. II, No 1, 1978. See also Wittfogel's *Oriental Despotism*, New Haven: Yale University Press, 1957. Wittfogel is one of the rare theorists who understands some of the implications of the 1914 War-Credits Vote for Marxism. He writes (Pages 181-182): "In the case of Russia, bureaucratic absolutism suffered a mortal blow from outside only 1917. Prior to this a marginal Oriental despotism adjusted successfully to the conditions of an advancing industrialization." Section 6c of Oriental Despotism, "The Extraordinary Staying Power of Tsarist Bureaucracy" goes a long way towards undermining the popular notion that Russia was becoming capitalist after 1905, a point to which we shall return.
32 Juergen Habermas, "Zur philosophischen Diskussion um Marx und den Marxismus," in *Theorie und Praxis: Sociophilosophische Studien,* Neuwied and Berlin: Luchterhand, 1963, p. 268. This is not the same book as the English-language *Theory and Practice* from Beacon Press.
33 On "semi-Asiatic Russian barbarism" Hoselitz and Blackstock, eds., *The Russian Menace to Europe*, Free Press of Glencoe, 1953. On the structure of European reaction, see below. On how to destroy the barbarism and break the reaction, see Marx's *Kapital*, Frankfurt/M-Berlin: Ullstein, 1969, K. Korsch, ed., page 659 (*Capital*, Vol. 1, New York, International Publishers, 1967, page 714): "As everyone knows . . . . in actual history, force (Gewalt) plays the greatest role."
34 At the outbreak of the war, Marx was clearly enthusiastic about the prospect of a Prussian victory. In the famous note of 20 July 1870 he wrote to Engels: "If the Prussians win . . . the centralization of the state power will be useful for the centralization of the working class. Moreover, German preponderance will cause the center of gravity of the workers' movement to be still more definitely shifted from France to Germany, and it is only necessary to compare the movement in the two countries from 1866 to now to see that the German working class is superior both theoretically and in organization to the French."

i

the German military victory would accelerate industrial development and hence the creation of an industrial working class, there can be little doubt his support of war against Czarist despotism, the social force Marx correctly identified as the most reactionary in the world, would have been unqualified.(Indeed a real critique of the SPD and the War Credits Vote of August 4, 1914 might question the momentary hesitancy of the SPD in voting the war credits and query why no pro-war agitation[35] had been carried on by the working-class party.

In a pithy and doubtless accurate statement, Boris Nicolaievsky and Otto Maenschen-Helfen sum up the Marxist attitude on war with Russia in *Karl Marx: Man and Fighter*[36]: "Marx shrunk at nothing when it came to striking a blow at Russian Czarism." What we have described as the very likely Marxist response to World War I, i.e., unconditional support to the Central Powers, falls easily within the broad parameters of "shrink at nothing."

The Leninist-Stalinist campaign to obscure this situation has proceeded with a two-pronged (and extraordinarily successful) tactic. The first prong consisted of pure stealth: the attempt to bury Marx's concept of the "semi-Asiatic barbarism" of Russian Oriental despotism.[37] Thanks primarily to Wittfogel, this flank has disintegrated, and at this point all serious Marx critics are conversant with the theory of Oriental despotism as well as the main thrust of Marx's political activity in the 1850s, political activity not aimed directly at organizing the Western working class to assume political power but rather to expose the collusion of Russian Oriental despotism with

---

35 Regarding the question of open pro-war agitation, see Engels' letter to August Bebel of 13 October 1891 (*Marx-Engels Werke*, hereinafter *MEW*, 38, pages 174-176), wherein Engels expresses his hope that the social-democrats will come to be "the only actually energetic war party" (*die einzige wirkliche energische Kriegspartei*). Bebel himself achieved a very high level of understanding of the nature of the Russian menace to Europe, as evidenced by his Marxist conception of a "war of annihilation" (*Vernichtungskrieg*) against Russian bureaucratic state slavery. In his letter to Engels of 12 Septembrr 1891, Bebel stated: "A war of annihilation must be declared; Czarism and its appendage must be overthrown; to defeat from without and to exterminate (*vernichten*) Czarism must become the express purpose of the war." Although various sophomores may detect hints of racialism or patriotism in Bebel's statement, it is in fact based on the clear recognition that until the "Gendarme of Europe" (Russia) is eliminated, working-class ascendancy is impossible. Bebel's unmistakable Marxist stand provides quite a contrast with Karl Kautsky in the war; by 1915 Kautsky had already embarked on his utopian quest to attempt to restore pre-1914 conditions in Europe, i.e., stop the combat before the Russian system was destroyed.
36 Nicolaievsky and Maenschen-Helfen, 1976, page. 247.
37 K.A. Wittogel, *Oriental Despotism,* Reference 1 above, Chapter 9.

British capital and French Bonapartism.[38] breaking up the latter combination would greatly accelerate the growth of the former movement. He even indicated that Russian Oriental despotism precipitated the U.S. Civil War.[39]

The second prong of the Bolshevists' strategy to block understanding of the politics of World War I and the genesis of their own movement was the theory of "Imperialism". The main function of this amorphous theoretic construction was to discredit Marx's strategy of what could be called "instrumental exploitation of the nation state." [40] How a Marx who could block with Bismarck against the land of 1789, the Ottoman Empire against the Greek independence movement, and the Habsburgs against the Italian national independence movement would hesitate to bloc with anyone against "semi-Asiatic barbarism" could not be explained and hence had to be explained away.

It is in this second area, the attack upon Marx's position of instrumental/tactical use of the nation state to undermine (or preferably destroy) regressive social formations, that Rosa Luxemburg is encountered. The argument of her *Junius Broschure* [41](April, 1916) closely parallels that of Lenin in his writings on the Second International . [42] To be sure, it is an

---

[38] This strategy is exemplified in *The Story of the Life of Lord Palmerston*, a collection of eight articles in *The People's Paper*, Oct.-Dec., 1953. These articles discuss Palmerston's "sinister policy" of arranging wars (including losing wars for England, if need be) as buffers against internal and (especially) external threats to Russian despotism. Marx's relation with British Tory politician David Urquhart, discussed most fully in *Herr Vogt* (see Reference 37 below) pages 474 and 475 is also important in this regard.

[39] Marx discusses the initiation of the United States Civil War in his pamphlet *Value, Price and Profit*, New York, International Publishers, 1976 (combined with *Wage Labour and Capital*) page 20: ". . . Russia, if we are to believe Mr. Urquhart, prompted the Civil War in the United States because her agricultural exports were crippled by the Yankee competition in the markets of Europe." Usually Marx is less restrained in his praise of Urquhart than in this passage. The interested student should consult, in addition to the passage cited in Reference 31 above Marx' letters to Engels of 22 April 1854 and to Lasalle of 2 June 1860 respectively.

[40] The difference between Marx and his opponents on the "left" on this issue is the difference between political action and "direct" action. Nicolaievsky and Maenschen-Helfen note here that (Nicolaievsky and Maenschen-Helfen, 1976, pages 319-320): ". . . Marx . . . regarded war as a factor in historical growth and in some circumstances a factor of historical advance. Whether a particular war were really the latter or not and what attitude the proletariat should adopt towards it were questions to be decided on the merits of a particular case."

[41] Rosa Luxemburg, *The Mass Strike: The Political Party & the Trade Unions. And the Junius Pamphlet.* New York: Harper Torchbooks, 1971. Hereinafter, Rosa Luxemburg, 1971.

[42] V.I. Lenin, *The War and the Second International,* New York: International Publishers, 1932. Hereinafter, Lenin, 1932.

undeniably pacifist revulsion at the carnage that motivates her condemnation of the working-class war effort[43] - unlike Lenin's covert sympathy for the authority patterns of the "Tartarized" Czarist state. But it is in any case on this latter ground , the political position that there was no moral choice for socialists between the Central Powers and the Russian Oriental despotism/British capital axis, that those leftists who still maintain the War Credits vote of the SPD was a "betrayl of socialist principles" must stand. In the following the controversy surrounding both issues – the politics of "Asiatic" Czarism (or "Czarist autocracy" as Marx would sometimes call it) and the theory of modern Imperialism – will be briefly sketched. Despite the separate treatment, the issues are part of the same core problematic; in fact the theory to be presented here is that the analytically specious and politically revisionist theory of Imperialism advanced by Rosa Luxemburg and Lenin, as well as the wide current of sympathy and support it enjoys to this day, are products of (among other things) an inadequate comprehension of the theory of Oriental despotism.

"Asiatic" Russia and Europe

a. *Herr Vogt*

" . . *'Vogt'* . . . is certainly the
best polemical work you have
ever written . . . ."

Frederick Engels to Marx,
9 December 1860

Marx's main analysis of the structure of the European reaction of his day unfolds not in the occasionally-read *Story of the Life of Lord Palmerston* but rather the obscure *Herr Vogt*.[44]

---

43 Rosa Luxemburg, 1971, pages 99-101.
44 Marx, *Herr Vogt*, Berlin: *MEW* 14, Dietz Verlag, 1974. Hereinafter Marx, *Herr Vogt*. Originally published at London in November of 1860. Engels states in his letter to Marx of 19 December 1860 that ". . . 'Vogt' . . . is certainly the best polemical work you have ever written. It is simpler in style than the Bonaparte pamphlet and yet, where necessary, every bit as effective" (*MEW* 30, page 129). The volume is mentioned (but not discussed) in David McLellan, *Karl Marx: His Life and Work*, New York:Harper Torchbooks, 1973, pages 314-315. McLellan advances the bromidic interpretation that Marx' opposition to Russia was an idiosyncratic personality trait rather than the heart of Marxist politics. Franz Mehring, Peter Stadler, Fritz Raddatz and Saul Padover all mention (but do not discuss) *Herr Vogt* in their respective biographies of of Marx. In several of these cases there is clear evidence that the biographer had never read *Herr Vogt*. Such a stricture does not apply to Maximilien Rubel, who flatly rejects the "personality" perspective on the book, stating in his *Marx/Engels: Die russische Kommune. Kritik eines Mythos* (Munich: Carl Hanser Verlag, 1972, page 330): "This little-read book is more than a personality statement " . . :. Hereinafter, Rubel, 1972.

The latter, disparaged by critics such as David McLellan as a personality attack, is in reality an extended treatment of Russo-European relations through the medium of a political and intellectual biography of the Czarist/Bonapartist police agent Carl Vogt.[45] For hundreds of pages the book related Russian foreign policy to imperatives of preservation of the Orientally despotic service state of Czarist Russia. In the decisive Chapter 8, "Dâ-Dâ Vogt and his Studies", such themes as the Russians' use of foreign policy to delay (*vertagen*) internal revolution, the progressive role of the Ottoman and Habsburg Empires in slowing the expansion of Russian despotism into Europe, Marx' admiration for British parliamentary Russophobe David Urquhart, the collabation of Louis Bonaparte and Pamerston with the Czar, as well as the socially regressive "emancipation" of the Russian serfs, are adumbrated. This last event, lauded effusively by Lenin, Marx describes as follows[46] "In any case the emancipation of the serfs *as conducted by the Russian regime* would would increase the aggressive power of Russia one hundred times over. The obvious purpose of it is the perfection of autocracy . . . . Just as Max Weber was to conclude that the Russian state "reforms" adopted in the wake of the 1905 Revolution actually strengthened Czarist despotism and made the development of capitalism even more unlikely in Russia [47] Marx concluded that the "emancipation" of the serfs begun in 1859 (proclaimed in 1861) would "increase one hundred fold" (*ums hundertfache steigern*) the virulence of Czarist despotism. This state of affairs, Marx asserted, was of European significance, not only because it had European after-effects but because it was in part directed by and to Europe. Specifically, Marx described a triumvirate of Victorian (Palmerston) Britain, Bonapartist France, and Russian "barbarism"; the Triple Entente,

---

45 Marx' insinuation that Vogt was a paid Bonapartist/Czarist police agent was fully confirmed at the time of the French provisional government of 1870, wherein payment receipts from the French secret police to Vogt (with Vogt's counter-signature affixed!) were recovered and published. This is conceded in McLellan (Reference 37 above), Edward's book on the Paris Commune (Reference 27 above), and in Peter Stadler, *Karl Marx: Ideologie und Politik,* Zürich, 1966, page 100. Despite all the ballyhoo, one should not be distracted by Marx' success in detecting the presence of a police agent; Marx' attack on Vogt was a means to the end of exposing the broader character of Anglo-Russian statecraft, not attacking an isolated individual. Marx unambiguously states in the Foreword to *Herr Vogt* that he is polemicizing against a party "that represents an entire direction" (*das eine ganze Richtung repräsentiert*), not one agent.
46 Marx, *Herr Vogt,* pages 497-498. Those with access to the 1860 original of *Herr Vogt* will find this critically-important passage on page 75 of that volume. There is a copy in the British Museum (now called the British Library) reading room.
47 Max Weber, "*Russlands Übergang zum Scheinkonstitutionalismus*" ("Russia's Transition to Phoney Constitutionalism") in Max Weber, *Gesammelte Politische Schriften.* Türingen: J.C.B. Mohr, 1971. Hereinafter, Weber, 1971.

diplomatically sanctified in 1912, that could be clearly seen operating in the 1850s. The destruction of this political combination, a combination disturbed (to put it mildly) by the German army in 1914, Marx sees as the chief political task of socialists in Europe.[48]

b. Germany and the Structure of Russo-European Relations

"... Russian diplomacy ... in Europe
is by no means limited to purely
diplomatic operations."

Marx, *New York Herald Tribune*,
7 April 1857

---

[48] Marx, Herr Vogt, page 506 as well as Chapter 8, "Dâ-Dâ Vogt and his Studies", in general. As *Herr Vogt* was going to press, Marx boasted that he had been agitating for a German-led world revolutionary war to destroy Russia for at least twelve years. In a letter to Lasalle of 15 December 1860 (*MEW* 30, page 565) Marx writes: "I think you are deceiving yourself concerning our relation to Russia. The perspective which Engels and I have developed is totally independent, and, I can say, labouriously (*muehsam*) developed through many years of studying Russian dipomacy. One indeed hates Russia in Germany, and we had already proclaimed the war against Russia as the revolutionary mission of Germany in the first issue of the *Neue Rheinische Zeitung*." There is little ambiguity to be found in this passage in which Marx once again re-affirms the ancient internationalist socialist goal of attempting to precipitate world war against Russian Oriental despotism led by the German state. The statement is important for another reason, namely, the weight Marx (and Engels) attached to the study of Russia. To this day many reputable commentators regard Marx as solely a critic of capitalism. How Marx could devote "labourious" study "over many years" (*vieljaehriges*) to a topic he regarded as being secondary in importance is left unexplained. Also left unexplained is Marx' startling announcement in *Herr Vogt* that he had prepared "a comprehensive work" (*einer ausfuerhrlichen Arbeit*) on Russia (Marx, *Herr Vogt,* page 474): "From a comprehensive work on this topic I have hitherto published only the introduction under the title "Revelations of the Diplomatic History of the 18*th* Century") (*Von einer ausfuehrlichen Arbeit ueber diesen Gegenstand habe ich nur die Einleitung drucken lassen unter dem Titel "Revelations of the Diplomatic History of the 18th Century."*). It is interesting to compare what Marx really said here with the "doctored" translation of the text published by the Leninist-Stalinist publishing house International Publishers. On page 7 of the "Publisher's Note" to *The Secret Diplomatic History of the 18th Century* and *The Story of the Life of Lord Palmerston* (1969), Marx's statement is rendered: "I want to devote to this subject a detailed study to which I have so far published only the introduction under the title "Revelations of the Diplomatic History of the Eighteenth Century." The phrase "I want to devote" is entirely gratuitous – in fact a fabrication. Furthermore, the phrase "a detailed study to which I have so far published" is grammatically ackward. The correct preposition is of course "from." What do these two distortions have in common? They are both designed to block recognition of the fact Marx had already written a comprehensive work on Russia. Such are the tactics used by the admirers of the Russia Revolution of 1917 to attempt to dilute the revolutionary politics of Marx; such is also a reason why so many commentators think Marx to be exclusively a critic of capitalist political economy.

Although a fair treatment of this topic would require several large octavo volumes, its general character may be indicated here. Basically, the two major capitalist powers, Britain and France, entered into a union with Czarist despotism because the former two powers, owing to the requirements of bourgeois "formal rationality" ("legal rationality"), could not internally generate a police force sufficiently terroristic to induce the political docility in the workforce the respective national ruling classes regarded as desirable. Of necessity, the German national state had to be excluded from this alignment; of necessity, the growth and development of German unity imperiled the combination. The unification of the Reich in 1871 and the industrial boom which followed (a development fully verifying Marx's predictions at the outbreak of the Franco-Prussian War): 1) blocked Czarist expansion westward; 2) confirmed the preeminent decline of Britain as the world's leading industrial power; 3) confronted the French with the most rapidly evolving military potential in the world; and most importantly 4) confronted European reaction with a "proletarian nation" - the largest, most sophisticated and most cohesive trade-union and working-class movement on the planet: the SPD. The SPD (Social Democratic Party of Germany) was more than 1000% larger than the next largest labour party in Europe.[49] Unlike the British Labour Party which exhibited an inability to develop general ideas which in many ways typifies Anglo-Saxon culture, or the French Socialist Party (SFIO), which also had no integral programmatic thrust, the German Party had a coherent ideological framework of action – Marxist socialism. The roots of this superiority in size and sophistication were not, however, to be found in remote cultural factors, but in the process of creating an industrial working class.

---

[49] The figures for the French and British parties (both well under 100,000 members) and the SPD (over 1,000,000 members) are given in W.H. Maehl, *German Militarism and Socialism*, Nebraska Wesleyan Press, 1968. The terms "proletarian nation" as well as "struggle against British plutocracy" are attributed to Eduard David. With these statistics it is not difficult to understand why the SPD dominated the 2nd International. It is also not difficult to understand why the "failure of the 2nd International" is a myth; the dominant group took the "correct" position. The purpose of the International was not to prevent war but rather but rather to advance the interests of the working class. Of course it does not take much imagination to come up with a policy that would have served the working class *and* prevented the war. The International should have declared that in case of war it would call for a general strike in Orientally-despotic aligned countries and 100 percent support for the war effort of the other side. Under such conditions the City of London would probably not have launched the conflagration in 1914.

The unprecedented intensity of German industrialization in the late nineteenth and early twentieth century became the determining factor in European political alignments at a time when these alignments were the center of world politics. The geo-political fortuity of confronting Russian territorial ambition and French state power, the historical fortuity of confronting British hegemony in Europe, but above all the socio-economic fortuity of confronting capitalism with its most powerful internally-generated opponent all combined to place Wilhelmian Germany, despite the will of most of its leaders, in an ideal position to violently disrupt the Triple Entente/Orientally despotic structure of reaction in Europe in 1914.

c. The Entente (Allied) Struggle
   to Make the World Safe for Despotism
   (Safe from Social Democracy)

"The Russians want to utilize . . . the dipilomatic union with France. Bebel and I have been carrying on correspondence concerning this, and we are of the opinion that if the Russians begin a war . . . we should be attacking the Russians and their allies a loutrance, no matter who these allies may be. If Germany is beaten, we will be beaten with her."

Frederick Engels (Letter to Sorge, 24 October 1891)

" . . . as opposed to the French Republic, which is in the service of the Russian Czar, German socialism represents the proletarian revolution unconditionally."

Frederick Engels (In *Die Neue Zeit*), Vol. X; 1891-1892)

"The people must be made to understand that a war of France in alliance with Russia against Germany above all is a war against the strongest and most militant socialist party in Europe."

Frederick Engels (Letter to A. Bebel, 29 September 1891[50])

The pre-war manuevers of British and French capital to preserve Czarist despotism and to defuse and defeat such liberation movements as existed inside Russia, a policy which was the logical concomitant of the diplomatic strategy of isolating Germany, at times entered the realm of the ingenious.

Historian R.D. Charques, in his volume *A Short History of Russia*,[51] records one such incident: "Less than two months before the Duma was to meet an event occurred which prepared the ground for a decisive stroke of government policy. On April 3, 1906, agreement was reached on the terms of the French loan of more than 2,000 million francs – the largest foreign loan which Russia had ever contracted . . . (the loan) . . . ensured the government's independence of the Duma and all its works for some time to come."

---

50 Engels' letter to Bebel of 29 September 1891 (MEW 38, pages 159-162) constitutes his most important statement on the nexus of the Wilhelmian state and the world social-democratic revolution and fully repays the most careful study. Engels comments that "So much appears certain to me. If the Germans (w*ir*) are defeated . . . the door is wide open for a war of revenge in Europe for years. If the Germans win, the social-democratic party will directly assume state power (*so kommt unsere Partei ans Rudder*) The victory of Germany is, therefore, the victory of the revolution " For those who accept the Marxist "Gendarme of Europe" theory, Engels' interpretation is almost inevitable. The only apparent flaw is the idea that the SPD would really have had a chance to govern Germany following a decisive victory for the Central Powers; the orthodox "gendarme" theory points to the conclusion that once the Russian political culture had been truly destroyed the era of the European nation-state would have ended almost immediately and the battered remnants of the world reaction would have been confronted by a united socialist Europe. Things turned out quite differently, of course. Although the Central Powers' military defeat of the Russians produced a partial extrusion of the Eurasian element in Russian political culture, it was insufficient to truly annihilate it, and in October of 1917 the Bolshevik Party was successful in executing a "Re-Russification" (de-Westernization) from above. However, this partial extrusion, even the most temporary defeat of Russia in 1917, produced the most intensive revolutionary wave Europe has ever seen. Unfortunately the first signs of the liberation of Europe from the Russian Yoke were so spectacular that the overall war effort of the Central Powers began to be disrupted.

51 R.D. Charques, *A Short History of Russia*, New York: Dutton, 1956, pages 226-227.

As events turned out, this "sacking of the Duma" by French capital soon became superfluous; the Russian revolt of 1905 had been so thoroughly crushed that the third Duma was a virtual rubber stamp for the Czar – a sham parliamentary appendage reminiscent of the post-1917 Bolshevik parliaments. The magnitude and boldness of the French effort are nonetheless noteworthy because they illustrate the depth of the integration of Asiatic Russia into Western capital and vice versa. Marx's aversion to Russia was more than an abstract revulsion at the degradation of man under despotic rule; it was also grounded in the realization that Czarist despotism undergirded subtler forms of repression *inside* civilized countries while it drew sustenance from these countries' most degenerate elements. This is the basis of the polemic against the Russophilism of Palmerston and Louis Bonaparte in *Herr Vogt*. On either ground, the general character of Russian barbarism in 1914, or the specific politico-diplomatic network outlined in *Herr Vogt*, the actions of the majority socialists in giving all-out support for the German war effort are unassailable from the perspective of Marxism. What, by contrast, was the attitude of Rosa Luxemburg and Lenin?

Origins and Function of the Leninist Stalinist
Theory of Imperialism in World War I:
"Inter-Imperialist Rivalry" as an
Ideological Ruse for Anti-Working-Class Politics

". . . Marx . . . regarded war as a
factor in historical growth and
. . . in historical advance."

Boris Nicolaievsky and Otto
Maenschen-Helfen in
Karl Marx: Man and Fighter (Ref. 33)

ROSA LUXEMBURG

A. *The Junius Brochure*[52]

1. Rosa Luxemburg's Theory of Oriental Despotism

Rosa Luxemburg's failure to understand the political context of World War I in Central Europe is probably less excusable than that of Lenin. While Lenin's references to Asiatic despotism in Russia were often Aesopian, ambiguous or sly[53], Rosa Luxemburg appears well-acquainted with the topic. Thus "Russian despotism" is repeatedly described (pages 113, 117, 123); the "Oriental" problem is discussed (page 137); "Asiatic Turkey" is mentioned (page 137); even the orthodox Marxist term "Oriental despotism" makes it appearance in the context of a discussion of Hither Asia (Asia Minor). Unfortunately this theoretic acumen comes to naught when Rosa Luxemburg tries to frame a general analysis from which political conclusions can be drawn; her main use o the concept of Oriental despotism consists of applying it to Ottoman Turkey, not Russia.[54] In a conspicuous revision of Marx, she discards the idea that the Ottoman Empire played a constructive role in containing Czarist autocracy. A passing reference to Marx's writings on the Crimean War, writings which first outlined his concept of Ottoman/Czarist relations, is made (page 141); however the pronouncements on the topic in *Herr Vogt* were apparently unknown to her.

2. Rosa Luxemburg's Theory of the Evolution of Czarist State and Society, 1859-1905.

Some of Rosa Luxemburg's comments on the increasing socio-economic integration of Russia and Europe in the late nineteenth century would, if taken in isolation, be almost prophetic. Thus we read (pages 164-165): "Russian absolutism is now subsidized by the Western European bourgeoisie . . . French money is rolling to Petersburg to feed a regime that would long ago have breathed its last without this life-giving juice . . . Russian Czarism is today no longer the product

---

[52] Rosa Luxemburg, 1971. All page references in the text are to this edition. Against his own inclinations, M. Rubel is forced to concede that *The Junius Brochure* became a foundation stone of Stalininst ideology. In the 1928 Kremlin attack on the "Gendarme" interpretation led by Stalin himself, the arguments of *The Junius Brochure* figured prominently (Rubel, 1972, page 350). It seems the Georgian butcher was particularly enamored with Rosa Luxemburg;s rhetoric about "competition for foreign markets" as an alleged cause of the war.
[53] K.A. Wittfogel, *Oriental Despotism* (Reference 1, above), Chapter 9.
[54] Rosa Luxemburg, 1971, page 137.

of Russian conditions; its root lies in the capitalist conditions of Western Europe . . . ". Regrettably, these promising observations are advanced in the context of basically faulty analysis. The fundamental question of capitalist/despotic relations in the pre-World War I period was this: What was the political intent and character of the developmental aid to the ancient despotisms from the newer, industrialized nations? Was the aid designed to accelerate the self-emancipation of the toiling masses (or better: state slaves) in the ancient regimes, provoking revolution in the East and thereby unleashing renewed revolution in the West? Or was the aid designed to streamline, protect and extend the total terror of Oriental despotism so as to maintain a political gendarme for the Western working class? In short, was capitalist influence wielded to undermine or strengthen Czarist despotism? If the latter case holds, was the capitalist structure of world reaction threatened by the German counter-attack on Czarist despotism in 1914? Rosa Luxemburg's analysis hinges on the belief that despite its own best efforts, Western capital had virtually transformed Russia into a capitalist nation by 1914.

Thus we are told "the new Russia of the Great Revolution of 1905" (page 163) is a new Russia; "the new Western European root is growing stronger and stronger" (page 165). Rosa Luxemburg's revision of Marxist politics, a revision she freely concedes (pages 165, 195), consists of a rejection of Marx's doctrine of the immutability of the Tartarized despotic service state of the Czar sketched in *Herr Vogt* and elsewhere.

3. Max Weber's Theory of the Evolution of Czarist State and Society, 1859-1905

Rosa Luxemburg was not alone in advocating the idea of the mutability of Russian Oriental despotism in the pre-World War I era, and it was for the purpose of laying such utopian fancies to rest for good and all that Max Weber devoted several magisterial essays, in particular "On the State of Bourgeois Democracy in Russia" (February 1906) and "Russia's Transition to Phoney

Constitutionalism" (August 1906).⁵⁵ The latter "review", a 246-page dissection of among other things the political program of the Russian "Constitutional Democrats", takes up the thesis that the upshot of he Revolution of 1905 was to weaken the Czarist apparatus state, and shreds it pitilessly. Although Weber was not so foolish as to deny the "uncanny" economic changes Russia had undergone since 1861, the conclusion of his detailed empirical analyses was that the despotic Russian bureaucracy was more firmly entrenched ever following the successful supression of the 1905 revolt. According to Weber, the "ever-stronger state bureaucracy" (page 72) had by 1906 "definitely rationalized autocracy throughout all areas of internal politics" (page 79); the "uncontrollable arbitrary power of the state bureaucrats" (page 72) had sharply accentuated "the defenselessness of the monarch" (page 79); "bureaucratic interests are united in a power trust extending to all organs of government" (page 79); the "rationalization of bureaucracy in Russia" has resulted in the "definitive establishment of the centralized domination of the modernized bureacracy" (page 78).⁵⁶

The "police-state absolutism" (page 106) which permits the bureaucracy to utilize "the most cunning means of the most tricky deceit" (page 109) means that "sly Mongol insidiousness" (page

---

55 The amazingly pronounced convergence of Weberian and Marxist models of despotism has been noted by several critics. Bryan S. White in his *Marx and the End of Orientalism* (London: Allen and Unwin, 1978) writes (page 1): "Within sociology, Max Weber's theory of patrimonialism . . . has close analytical similarities with the Marxist concept of the Asiatic mode of production . . .". An example of the convergence would be *Russia under the Old Regime* (New York: Scribner's, 1974) by Harvard University historian Richard Pipes. From the overweening influence of the Tartar Yoke to the non-existence of Russian capitalism, Pipes' analysis of what he terms "Russia's patrimonial regime" serves to confirm what Marx by 1855 termed "Russo-Mongol barbarism." The discussion of the last point – the non-existence of Russian capitalism – is particularly effective. Pipes rejects the Leninist-Stalinist legend that capitalism or any approximation of it ever existed as the dominant social formation in Russia; he scores "the deceptive panorama of a flourishing capitalism painted by communist historians" (page 207). In addition Pipes provided the date – 14 August 1881 (page 305) – upon which the transition from the traditional to the modern (20ᵗʰ century) police state began in Russia. In sum, *Russia under the Old Regime* is a major contribution to the debate on pre-Bolshevik despotism.
56 However steep the decline of his intellectual powers during and after the Great War, the leading theorist of the 2ⁿᵈ International recognized the dimensions of Max Weber's achievement. In his 1927 two-volume truly magnum opus *Die Materialistische Geschichtsauffassung* (The Materialistic Conception of History) (Berlin: Verlag J.H.W. Dietz) Karl Kautsky paid full tribute to Max Weber: "Absolutely no one (*wohl niemand*) has so clearly grasped the difference between Orientally despotic states (*Staaten des orientalischen Despotismus*) as opposed to . . . the states of Continental Europe . . . as . . . Max Weber." In light of this *laudatio* it is scarcely surprising that Kautsky adds on the same page that Weber's work had provided him with "a series of insights" that were "extremely fruitful" for his research.

84) now enjoys free rein to promulgate its "politics of repression" (page 71). No wonder that Weber concludes that "the total power carried over from the Tartar Age" (page 33) will be permanently destroyed only through a *European* war." (page 56, emphasis in original). If Weber's analysis is even partly correct, the legion of history professors who describe the 1906-1917 Russian regime as a "constitutional monarchy" and "developing toward capitalism" should perhaps reconsider their position. In any case, Wittfogel seconds Weber's judgment in Chapter 9 of *Oriental Despotism* : "But all . . . eternal influences did not destroy the absolutist character of the state. The relations of the Tsarist bureaucracy to the forces of property . . . continued to be determined by conditions that had long ago been operative in traditional Russian society. And this relation was, and remained, a relation of absolute superiority . The masters of the despotic state apparatus .. . did not relinquish their total power . . . until 1917."

B. *Political Conclusions*

Rosa Luxemburg's position that the basic character of Russian despotism had changed in the pre-war period is both the lynch-pin of her political analysis and untenable. Although an embryonic industrial workforce was developing as a result of both long-time Czarist policy and penetration by Western capital, the attempt to use the lessons of Western politics in "Asiatic" Russia led directly tragi-comic results. The Bolshevist-Stalinist tendency to apply terminology from the French Revolution to Orientally despotic nations, a practice which became sickeningly familiar after 1917, is already visible in April 1915, the date when the *Junius Brochure* was completed. Thus in the course of an attempted "class analysis" of Russian conditions, the reader is informed that (page 166): "There was the difficulty of creating a class state for the supremacy of the modern bourgeoisie against the counter-revolutionary opposition of the bourgeoisie as a whole. To the onlooker it would seem that the Russian Revolution was doomed to failure because it was a proletarian revolution with bourgeois duties and problems, or, if one wishes, a bourgeois revolution waged by proletarian methods . . . ". And so the two main actors in the Russia drama are seen to be the barely-existing proletariat and a bourgeoisie which never existed as a ruling class in Russia. The apparatus-state autocracy on the other hand, the group plainly identified as the foundation of Russian social and political life by Marx [57] is left out. In this case the product of an inadequate comprehension (or perhaps a political rejection) of the theory of Oriental despotism is a faulty critique indeed.

V.I. Lenin

A. *The War and the Second International*

"Which of two warring nations gained
the victory could not possibly be a matter
of . . . indifference . . . to the proletarian
movement."

Boris Nicolaievsky and Otto Maenschen-Helfen,
in *Karl Marx: Man and Fighter*

Lenin, though burdened by neither the ingeniousness nor the sensitivity of Rosa Luxemburg,[xiv] proved himself far more sophisticated tactically than his Polish comrade; the (historically) crudely effective essays "The Collapse of the Second International" and "The War and Russian Social Democracy" ignore the question of "Asiatic despotism"[58] in Russia or any other place, a Bolshevik ploy to this day. Lenin alludes to the avowed struggle of German and Austrian workers against Czarism and criticizes Russia as "reactionary and barbarous" (Lenin, 1932, page 57) but

---

[57] Marx, *Herr Vogt*, page 498. Rosa Luxemburg, like Lenin, is utterly revisionist in rejecting the Marxist idea of the cultural stationariness of Asiatic (particularly Russian) society and is irresponsible for not explaining it. But a certain consistency is perceivable. This is less true of the aging Engels, who usually upheld the position of supporting war against Russia but had little difficulty maintaining at the same time that that Czarist society was steaming pell-mell for the Western camp. So exaggerated was Engels' estimation of the changes in late 19th-century Russia that M. Rubel was obliged to condemn his "naive and optimistic confirmation of capitalist progress in the Czarist empire" (Rubel, 1972, page 129). Such criticism could not be leveled at Weber, whose portrait of late Czarist society as dominated by an Asiatic-bureaucratic autocracy which had such puny facsimiles of capital as existed at the end of a very short tether indeed is easily the closest to that of the Marx of *Herr Vogt*. Thus: Rosa Luxemburg and Lenin are revisionists who nonetheless deduce their tactics more or less rigorously from their sociology; the Engels of advanced years is a genuine eclectic who usually upholds the long-standing tactic of war against Russia while moving away from the sociological analysis of an unbridgeable gulf between Russia and the West which made the tactic so viable in the first place; and lastly *Weber* appears the stridently orthodox Marxist, affirming both the age-old character of Czarist autocracy and the impossibility of transforming it short of war.

[58] K.A. Wittfogel, *Oriental Despotism*, Chapter 9. See also his article in *The Soviet Union: The Seventies and Beyond*, B.W. Eisenstat, ed., Lexington, Mass.: D.C. Heath, 1975.

the end result of the perfunctory commentary is to shove the question of Russian socio-political structure into the background. In its place the theory of "inter-imperialist rivalries" is outlined, a theory to be elaborated further in *Imperialism: The Highest Stage of Capitalism*. Lenin goes on to repeat the thesis of the *Junius Brochure* that there is nothing to choose between the Central Powers and the Oriental despotism/Western Capital axis (ibid): "Neither of the groups of belligerent countries is behind the other in robberies, bestialities, and endless brutalities of war . . . . The bourgeoisie of each country strives . . . to extol the significance of 'its own' national war and to assert that it strives to vanquish the adversary, not for the sake of robbery and the seizure of lands, but for the sake of liberating all the other peoples except its own."

Even on the narrow point of atrocities and "bestialities", the Leninist analysis runs into the ground. As historian Carrol Quigley has documented[59], the Central Powers simply could not compete with the Czarist/British Capital axis for viscerally mendacious propaganda. This situation flowed not so much from an inherently defective British national character (although the term "Perfidious Albion" was not cut from whole cloth) but rather constituted one of the consequences *inside* British society of partial social integration with structural barbarism.

Lenin's second point is also revealing. Although the "Czarist monarchy" is mentioned, the real analysis is that "the bourgeoisie of each country" is in charge. It shall be left to conspiracy theorists and psycho-historians to determine who much of this distortion was deliberate; such is ultimately a question of individual psychology. More important is the school of *social* psychology spawned by Leninist analyses of the response of the Central European working class to the Triple Entente assault upon civilization in 1914.

*B. Neo-Leninist Social Psychology and the
Working-Class Response to the First
World War: Some Aspects*

The claim has several times been advanced that Marx's overall critique of Oriental despotism in Russia as well as the detailed analysis in *Herr Vogt* point to unqualified support for the war-credits vote of the SPD on August 4, 1914. If this be accepted, then those with a *Praxis* orientation will not delve too deeply into the motives of the combatants who sought to block (and if possible reverse) the march of Tartar barbarism westward. Marx states in his letter to Lasalle of 2 June 1860 (*MEW*): " . . . (I)n a war against Russia it makes no difference to me whatsoever (*ist mir ganz gleichgültig*) . . . whether your neighbor shoots as Russians from national-patriotic or revolutionary motives."

As the reader might expect by now, Boris Nicoialevsky and Otto Maenchen-Helfen evince clear understanding of the situation in *Karl Marx: Man and Fighter*: " . . . [W]hen it came to attacking Russia, Marx was willing to enter into a alliance with the devil himself." But despite all of this, despite Marx's relentless denigration of subjective intent of historical actors vis-á-vis the

---

59 Carrol Quigley, *Tragedy and Hope,* New York: MacMillan, 1967, page 263.

objective historical consequences of actions, the fact virtually all major interpretations of the Marxism of the Second International and the German War-Credits vote are in part grounded in a vulgar social psychology of the motives of SPD deputies and the German working class justifies an aside.

The writings in this area will be invaluable for working out a class analysis of the relations of workers and intellectuals. The incredible radicalism of the German workers in rallying to support the war seems to have inspired the most intensive fit of class and status anxiety ever to afflict bourgeois intellectuals. Every move the class-conscious Central European proletariat [made] is "exposed" as a mask for irrational chauvinism. Thus Carl E. Schorske, in his highly-touted *German Social Democracy 1905-1917* [60] writes: (the) . . . elemental force of love of country was moving like a river of lava [sic – WFD] thrusting aside international traditions." Dieter Groh, author of the much-heralded *Negative Integration und revolutionärer Attentismus: Die deutsche Social-Demokratie am Vorabend des ersten Weltkrieges* (Negative Integration and Revolutionary Attentism: German Social Democracy on the Eve of the First World War) (Frankfurt/M, 1973) thought he perceived (page 673): "War hysteria, the psychological (sic) variant of the over-foaming (sic) war enthusiasm which broke out the same day . . . ".

Even a cursory examination of the publicity of the German working-class organizations at the outbreak of the war reveals a picture that has almost nothing in common with the "subrational nationalism" thesis prominent n the most prestigious interpretations. In reality quite another topic is at the center of attention in the socialist press: "Everywhere the same cry: against Russian despotism . . . . " (*Bielefelder Volkswacht,* 4 August 1914); " . . . (I)n the enemy whom wer are fighting in the East we are striking a blow at the foe of all civilization and progress . . . . The overthrow of Russia is synonymous with the victory of freedom in Europe." (*Halle Volksblatt,* 5 August 1914); " . . . (T)he Social Democrats since the fight is against Russian Blood-Czarism, against the perpetator of a million crimes against freedom and culture, will allow none to excel them in the fulfillment of their duty, in their willingness to sacrifice. Down with Czarism! Down with the home of barbarism!" (*Essener Arbeiterzeitung,* 5 August 1914); "You are fighting for the civilization of Europe . . . ". (*Rheinische Zeitung,* 5 August 1914).

---

60 Carl E. Schorske, *German Social Democracy 1905-1917*, New York: Harper and Row, 1972.

These quotes make it clear that a critically important factor in the response of the Central European working class and its institutions to the crisis of 1914 was a desire to defend civilization itself against Russian barbarism and its allies in the West. The dread of Russia exhibited by German workers (a phenomenon, by the way, which ends the argument whether social democrats or Bolsheviks had the best claim to the legacy of Marx) cannot be attributed solely to a proto-Nazi chauvinism but rather in large part to an unmistakable consciousness of the despotic character of the Czarist regime and its destructive role vis-á-vis anything enlightened, republican or authentically socialist. Even if this awareness was not fully articulated intellectually, the publicity shown above illustrates that the collective German proletariat ws definitely aware it was fighting an Asiatic despotism which contributed to reaction throughout the world. This dread of Russia, perhaps the single sentiment most likely to contribute to the longevity of Europe as a distinct geo-political and cultural entity, had roots which long pre-dated the rise of the industrial proletariat' it harkens back beyond the fear created by the Russian invasion of 1791, to the terror engendered by the Mongol invasion of Europe in the Thirteenth Century – the barbarism of the Asian horsemen left a permanent scar. No socialist could ever fault the Central European workers for wanting to avoid the fate of Kievan Russia, the remonstrances of Rose Luxemburg and Lenin notwithstanding.

ACKNOWLEDGEMENTS

Thanks to James T. Burnett for encouragement. Henry Pachter was kind enough to go over the manuscript at some length. Neither Burnett nor Pachter necessarily endorses the contentions made herein.

****

APPENDIX: Karl Renner's *Marxismus, Krieg und Internationale*

Up to now the main spokesman for pro-war, pro-Central Powers socialism has been Austrian social-democrat Karl Renner, author of *Marxism, War and the International: Critical Studies on the Public Problems of Scientific and Practical Socialism in and After the World War* (Stuttgart Dietz Verlag, 1917; in German). In Section 14, "Toward a Justification of the German Proletariat," Renner advances what amounts to a merely *tactical* justification of the SPD and the German War-Credits Vote of August 4, 1914, stating that the Czarist invasion of Central Europe and the social havoc it signified left German workers with no choice but to resist with the best means at hand, the German national state. Although true as stated, the argument is not fully compelling. The reason is that Renner has swallowed the Leninist rhetoric and theory of "Imperialism" virtually whole. The Leninist Imperialism position, a position which congealed at the outset of the war, posited a virtual convergence of social structures in Asia and Europe, i.e., that Russia was rapidly becoming (or had become) a Western, European, capitalist nation. If this were true, no compelling, proletarian internationalist rationale for fighting on one side or the other could be found. However – and here is the decisive point – if one side was grounded in what Marx variously termed "Russo-Mongolian barbarism", "Russian Oriental Despotism." "a despotism in Russia the likes of which Europeans cannot even imagine", and "a rule of systematic terror, devastation and wholesale massacre forming its institutions", then a persuasive *strategic* argument for all world citizens to support the Central Powers could have been advanced. Bu uncritically accepting the (implicitly unilinear) sociological assumptions of the Leninist model, Renner prevented himself from making a really strong case for pro-Central Powers Marxism.

If Renner's socialist rationale for the War-Credits vote is unconvincing, the same cannot be said for the analysis of Max Weber. Weber certainly outperforms Renner in this respect because he focuses directly upon Russian autocratic despotism as the key to understanding the origins and significance of the 1914 conflagration. In what may be one of the most analytically incisive comments on the German Social-Democrats and the War Credits Vote of August 4, 1914 ever made, Weber fully endorsed the SPD policy when he wrote in 1919 that: "He who has made himself acquainted with the state system of Czarism knows well that to the ends of the earth here was nothing to compare with its cunning means of degrading a people . . . . He knows also – as the German Social Democracy knew on August 4, 1914 – that a war against *this* system was a good war . . . ". in "On the Theme of War Guilt," (Reference 40, above).

Works Cited

NOTE: Works cited are from the main text only. The 1980 Appendix has its own citations.

Stefan Bollinger

Weltbrand, >>Urkatastrophe<< und linke Scheidewege. Fragen an den >>Grossen Krieg,<< 2014

Die Russen Kommen! Wie umgehen mit dem Ukrainekrieg? Über deutsche Hysterie und deren Ursachen. 2022

and Juha Koivisto, "Hegemonic Apparatus" in Historical Materialism 17 (2009).

Max Weber

German

Gesammelte Politische Schriften, 5th Edition, 1988, Johannes Winckelmann, Ed., 1988
Max Weber. Politik und Gesellschaft, Daniel Lehmann, Ed., 2006
Max Weber. Kürzere Politische Schriften. No editor. 2019

English

Weber. Political Writings. Peter Lassman and Ronald Speiers, Eds. Cambridge Press, 1994

OTHER

Hinnerk Bruhns, *Max Weber und der erste Weltkrieg*, 2007
William F. Drischler, "Marx and Russia. An Eight-Point Introductory Reconstruction," (1981) in William F. Drischler, Max Weber and the Slavs, 2019

William F. Drischler, "Max Weber and Russia." (1984) in William F. Drischler, Max Weber and the Slavs, 2019

William F. Drischler, "Marx's Best Polemic. Russo-Napoleonism and the Italian Question in *Herr Vogt*," in *Beiträge zur Marx-Engels-Forschung. Neue Folge,* 1994.

William F. Drischler, "Bismarck – Russian Agent in the Tartar Troika. Marx on the Rise of the Iron Chancellor," in *Beiträge zur Marx-Engels-Forschung. Neue Folge*, 1997

William F. Drischler, "Louis-Napoleon as Russo-Asiatic Agent. Marx's Revision of *The 18th Brumaire* in *Herr Vogt*," in *Beiträge zur Marx-Engels-Forschung*. Neue Folge, 1998

William F. Drischler, Max Weber & The Slavs, 2019

William F. Drischler, The Peace of Utrecht. Origins of Neo-Chinggisid International Relations Structures 1713-1998, 2022

Gwynne Dyer, The Shortest History of War, 2nd Printing 2022

Fritz Fischer, Germany's Aims in the First World War, 1967

Jürgen Habermas, "A Plea for Negotiations," in the *Suddeutsche Zeitung*, Feb. 14, 2023

Edith Hanke, et al., The Oxford Handbook of Max Weber, 2019

W.I. Lenin. Biographie. No author. East Berlin, 1970

Wolfgang J. Mommsen, *Max Weber und die Deutsche Politik 1890-1920*, 2nd ed. 1974.

Wolfgang J. Mommsen, *Max Weber. Zur Neuordnung Deutschlands. Schriften und Reden 1918-1920*, 1991

Hans-Peter Müller, *Max Weber. Eine Spurensuche*, 2020

Karl Palonen, "The Supranational Dimension in Max Weber's Vision of Politics," in E. Hanke et al., eds, The Oxford Handbook of Max Weber, 2019

RT [Russia Today]. "BRICS De-dollarization push gaining momentum – Jakarta," April 21, 2023

Anthony Sutton, Wall Street and the Rise of Hitler, 2010 Edition

Peter Wahl, "*Der Ukraine-Krieg und seine geopolitische Hintergründe. Hintergrundpapier Nr. 1, vom 18. März 2022 (Redakionsschluss),*" Attac AG Globalisierung und Krieg, Frankfurt/M, 2022

Gordon C. Wells and Peter Baehr, eds., "Introduction" to Max Weber. The Russian Revolutions, 1997

Afterword.
Species Boost and
Hegemony Loss Anxiety

In recent years Russian President Putin had made public references to evolutionary prospects for the human species in general. He has cautioned against those who – wedded to an increasingly obsolescent hegemony network – are in fact (and possibly self-consciously) – seeking to mislead the world public about potential ascent to a new, higher species Man, this in hopes of delaying such ascent.

Such constitutes yet another contemporary parallel to the situation in Continental Europe in August 1914. As suggested in the Appendix, if the German-led Central Powers in WWI had been able to secure a quick and decisive military victory over Czarist Russia, the Russo-Asiatic mode of production would have collapsed and the Anglo-Russian secret diplomacy state would have gone down with it, along with the Triple Entente and the Anglo-Saxon hegemony unit as well. A united socialist Europe in 1914 would have been poised to organize the liberation of the entire planet, i.e., bring about species boost. Although blocking species boost cannot be the only component of hegemony loss anxiety, it was surely part of the package for the Triple Entente's hidden controllers in August 1914, and it is surely part of the package today as the USA gracelessly, e.g., in the Solomon Islands, tries to fend off the ceaselessly-growing challenges to its longstanding global role.

Made in the USA
Columbia, SC
18 May 2023